THE TRAGEDIES
John Galt

Vocamus Editions
Guelph, Ontario

Published by Vocamus Press
© All rights reserved

Transcription and Footnotes by David J. Knight
© All rights reserved

Preface by Nick Ford
© All rights reserved

Cover image by Sona Mincoff
© All rights reserved

ISBN 13: 978-1-77422-022-1 (pbk)
ISBN 13: 978-1-77422-037-5 (ebk)

Vocamus Editions
130 Dublin Street, North
Guelph, Ontario, Canada
N1H 4N4

www.vocamus.net

2020

Lady Clytemnestrantonia MacMaddalen-Beth

Nick Ford

Preface

This drama is the sketch of dissipation, and as such, is offered to the public. It was written during the quarantine of lockdown in the late coronavirus epidemic, when I could contrive no better way of employing my attention.

With respect to the style, I consider the many plagiarismata of Shakespeare's more tedious pentametric colloquies, following Chaucer's, as if it were some canonical law, to be in as bad a taste as to imitate the quaint obsolescences peculiar to the Romantics of Mr. Galt's age (as if Spenser's medievalist absurdities were some extenuation), or in following the ancient Greek dramatic unities without employing an all-singing, all-dancing, chorus.

In producing this satire upon the tragedy of Mr. Galt having penned no fewer than five such, each one as dull as the next, I have made use of an economical conflation—a quintessential three-act Galt tragedy, one might say—for which I make no apology to modern Canadian readers with rather less time on their hands, than their early 19thC counterparts desperate for something—anything—newer to read, than last quarter's seed catalogue.

Nick Ford, Ludlow, 28th July 2020

Lady Clytemnestrantonia MacMaddalen-Beth

A Tragic Play in Three Acts
after the manner of
The late Mr. John Galt

Dramatis Personae

Lady Clytemnestrantonia, a Noblewoman cruelly used by Fate
Arsenica, her Nurse
The Duke
Valenzo and Lorendini, Two Gentlemen of Verona
Ferdinando and Seaton, Servants.

The stage represents a chamber in the palace and remains unchanged despite an infinity of scenes throughout all three acts.

Act I, Scene I

(Clytemnestrantonia and Arsenica).

C: Who is John Galt?

A: Why, Madam! Know you not
    This city of Guelph doth this day in his honour
    Keep solemn feast, to celebrate the founder?
    Banks will be clos'd, and no mail be deliver'd

By Canada Post. There'll be no waste collection
On Monday, and the service is delay'd
All week, by the Duke's strict ordinance. The Waste
Resource Innovation Centre shuts,
Whereby it, too, will keep the coming holiday.
All city buildings, libraries, and museums,
Will also bar their portals for the day:
So says the Mercury-Tribune, by my troth,
But as of yet, I cannot ascertain
That Guelph Transit will run upon the day.

C: But who, I say, is this John Galt? Pray answer.
But soft! Who knocks? There's someone at the door.
Go answer it instead, and, having answer'd
Straitway return and tell me who's without.
Go quickly, now. Away!

A: Madam, I go.

ACT I Scene I
(Clytemnestrantonia and Arsenica).

A: Madam, the Duke hath sent his servant here
Charged straitly to deliver you a message:
The which, he hath most faithfully discharged
In giving it to me, that I might, in my turn.
Place that same scroll into your hands,
That you might break apart the waxen seal,
And then, the silken riband once unloos'd,
Unbind its papery folds, and then divine
By reading its several characters there inscrib'd
(For you, Madam, can read, and I cannot)
The meaning and the portent of that missive

C: Give me the letter. Where's my paper-knife?

Lady Clytemnestrantonia MacMaddalen-Beth

A: 'Tis there, Madam, upon the mantelpiece.

C: Well, bring it here to me, then. Tell me now:
    You are a woman, knowing and observant.
    I wish we were in some secluded room,
    Where no intrusion might break in upon us.

A: We are, Madam, in the privacy of your house.

C: Ah! So we are. 'Tis well. Now, tell me truly —
    How did the servant look when you saw him?

A: Madam, he lookt like one that kens dread things
    That are invisible to mortal sight.
    Just like Paulina in the picture there,
    When told her love was not the God Anubis,
    Pale, agonized, almost foregone in mind.
    He looks not as a man on woman looks,
    But as a student pond'ring o'er a text.

C: 'Tis passing strange. Now let me read this letter.

A: The messenger of my lord the Duke's here still:
    Shall I bid him go, or wait on your reply

C: Pray bid him stay the while: give him to drink,
    And let the audience likewise, while I think.

(*Intermission*)

ACT II, Scene I

(Ferdinando and Arsenica).

F: Where's thy mistress?

A: Marry, she is gone
   Into her closet, that she might compose
   In thought-provoking solitude, a reply
   To the letter of your master my lord the Duke,
   And we are here so that no change of scene
   Unseemly may disturb the unities
   Of drama, as set forth in the *Poetics*
   Of Aristotle (and it saves on paint
   As well as on the playwright's imagination).
   Know you what the Duke's letter doth contain?

F: I do.

A: Say, what?

F: I may not tell.

A: Oh, fie!

F: Who asks no questions shall be told no lie.

ACT III, Scene I

(Clytemnestrantonia, Arsenica and Ferdinando).

C: Give this as my reply unto thy master.

F: Madam, I will.

A: I'll see thee to the door.

ACT III, Scene II

(The Duke, Clytemnestrantonia, Arsenica, Ferdinando, Seaton, Valenzo, Lorendini).

Lady Clytemnestrantonia MacMaddalen-Beth

C: My lord the Duke, you do this house much honour.

D: No thanks are due to me, my lady: strait
   Upon the commandment of this script, I come.

C: My letter did not summon you, my lord.

D: I mean the author of this script, John Galt.
   No more than he commands, may we perform;
   Nor stray beyond the boundaries prescribed
   By Aristotle's dramatic unity.
   Hence we are here, and may not elsewhere be.

C: Who is John Galt?

A: Why, Madam! Know you not?

C: No more than who these other people are,
   Save the servitor of my lord the Duke, Ferdinando,
   And of course, my lord the Duke himself.

A: And me, Madam, that suckled thee from infancy,
   Charged by the Duke, to raise thee up in secret,
   Far from Urbino's court, and from the jealousy
   Of the Duchess thy cruel step-mother (now deceased),
   That else had compassed thine untimely death.

C: You, the Duke—my father? Can this be?

L: And I, poor child, thy mother. Many a year
   Have I walked this world disguised in old man's weeds
   As the grave and reverend courtier, Lorentini.

V: And I, Count Valenzo, am thy brother, cast adrift
   In open boat on Amalfi's rocky shore
   By those that sought our downfall, but was found
   By humble fisher-folk, but through prowess

And strange adventures many, became an admiral
　　　Of the fleet of Venice's serene republic.

F: And I, Ferdinando, rightly am the son
　　Firstborn of the King of Naples. When I first
　　Beheld thee, fairest Clytamnestrantonia,
　　I left my principality, took service with the Duke,
　　Learning he was thy father, and hoped thus
　　To win thy father's favour, and thy hand.

D: This is a happy day! Let all rejoice!
　　Let drink be brought, and pledge Dame Fortune here!
　　So may these lovers' hands in matrimony be join'd,
　　And all be one united family!

S: So as you all have drunk the wine, know this:
　　I, Seaton, am thy bitterest enemy,
　　The brother of the late dead Duchess I,
　　Who in vengeful spite thy wine have all envenom'd,
　　Whereof now, too, I drink, my plan fulfill'd,
　　Th'executioner to avoid, now all are kill'd.

HAHAHAHAHAAAA!

　　　　　　(Curtain)

The Tragedies of MADDALEN, AGAMEMNON, LADY MACBETH, ANTONIA & CLYTEMNESTRA.

by John Galt

"Se ella è nato per fare tragedie, il suo sarà o peggiore o migliore od uguale." - Alfieri.[1]

London: Printed for Cadell and Davies. 1812.
W. Smith and Co. Printers, King Street, Seven Dials.

---

[1] Vittorio Alfieri (1749-1803), Italian dramatist and poet. This line appears in *Le opere postume di Vittorio Alfieri* Volume 1 (1809; page 53). Galt has "... il suo sará..." while the original is "... il suo sarà..."

Preface

John Galt

These Dramas are the sketches of pastime, and as such are offered to the public. MADDALEN was written in the Lazzaretto of Messina, to lighten the captivity of quarantine; CLYTEMNESTRA during a passage from Sardinia to Gibraltar; AGAMEMNON in the course of my voyage from that fortress to Ireland; ANTONIA, while obliged to perform a second quarantine in Cork harbour; and LADY MACBETH, at subsequent intervals, when I could contrive no better way of employing my attention. In compositions so hasty, polished correctness ought not to be expected. I think it would be easier to write others than to make these more worthy of perusal, by any application which I might exert; and I have printed them, because I do not think that they ought to be destroyed.

But although negligence of language be pardonable, the manner and subjects may provoke animadversion; and the names of AGAMEMNON, LADY MACBETH and CLYTEMNESTRA, are calculated to occasion mortifying comparisons. With respect to the style, I consider the characteristics of the British dramatic verse as having been fixed by Shakespear; and his successors, in my opinion, would shew as bad a taste in attempting to introduce a new manner, as in imitating the obsolete quaintness peculiar to the writers of his age. I have, therefore, endeavoured to adapt his simple and colloquial metres to modern modes of expression. But in the structure of the drama, I have ventured to preserve the unities of the Greek theatre, along with the natural circumstances and dialogue of the English; and I have chosen to divide the fable into three parts, (I know not why five should have been hitherto preferred,) and my text will be found to indicate without the aid of marginal notes, what should be the business of the stage. Whether these are actually improvements, experience must decide.

For the manner in which I have treated the often-rehearsed stories of AGAMEMNON and CLYTEMNESTRA, I make no apology. The former is a gross and detestable topic; and the latter is so truly horrible, that to have managed either without disgusting, will be no inconsiderable praise. The greatest poets have written on these subjects; and The ELECTRA of Sophocles is a hideous and inhuman exhibition.

For presuming to meddle with the awful mysteries of MACBETH, I have not one word to offer in extenuation. I thought the almost satanic character of the Lady, possessed traits of grandeur which might be so represented as to excite compassion; and the frame of Macbeth's mind afforded me an opportunity of introducing allusions to Scottish superstitions which Shakespear has not touched; and which are still, in a great measure, new to the poetry of the stage. The play is, in fact, an experiment; and as such, I wrote it with some degree of audacity both in thought and phraseology. It is the best or the worst in the volume.

With regard to the other two pieces, MADDALEN and ANTONIA; the first was undertaken to try whither such a person as the Dutchess, a character of meaner energies than the generality of those on whom the interest of the solemn drama is supposed essentially to depend, might be rendered capable of exciting a tragical degree of pathetic sympathy; and the second seemed to afford scope for new situations, and the means of embodying a class of observations, which, though not sufficiently popular for the stage, could only be intelligibly expressed in dramatic circumstances.

London, 19th April, 1812.[1]

---

1 The War of 1812 was declared June 18th.

[Galt's Errata. "-Page 4, line 5, for bedeck't read bedeck'd' page 37,[2] for Scene V. read Scene IX; page 35, line 4, for Approbrious read Opprobrious; page 53, line 9, for approbrious read opprobrious; page 32,[3] line 4, for threats read throats; page 99, line 14, for gratitude read ingratitude; page 120, line 7, for falsely, sad adorn'd read falsely sad, adorn'd; page 123, line 13, for Firth read Forth; page 130, line 22, for alm read alms; page 139, line 9, for heart read breast; page 177, line 12, for porticos read portico."][4]

---

[2] These page numbers refer to the original 1812 publication produced by Cadell and Davies.
[3] Mistake for 82 in the original 1812 text.
[4] All of these corrections have been made in the following text.

MADDALEN, A Tragedy

Characters.

VALDINI
LORENZO
DUKE
MADDALEN
DUTCHESS

The Stage represents a Saloon.

ACT I, Scene I

MADDALEN.

O wretched me! O dismal wedding day!
Break fated heart, and rather to the tomb
Let me be borne than to the bridal bed,
Incestuous to my soul. Valdini's wife!
Wife to the father of my lov'd Lorenzo!—
The sworn accepted husband of my heart.
What dire delusion drew me on to this?

Knew I not well my uncle's ruthless mind?
How could I hope, or on despair rely?
O deadly apathy! O mortal hour,
In which I put these gaudy trappings on,
And gave my hand. This faithless hand, so oft'
The glowing record of Lorenzo's passion,
Is to his father pledg'd, for love, for faith,
For all that ere I cherish'd for Lorenzo.
Ah hapless son! son? mine? my lover mine!

ACT I, Scene II

MADDALEN *and* LORENZO.

MADDALEN Ha! Lorenzo!

LORENZO You here! O Maddalen!

MADDALEN Leave me, go, go.—

LORENZO Ah rather on thy bier,
Unhappy fair, would I have seen thee laid,
Than with this bridal garnishing bedeck'd.

MADDALEN Despise, upbraid me; but in harsher terms,
That I may learn to be your step-mother.—
Recount my perjuries; recall the scenes,
Where we in childhood, innocent and free,
As th' infant Cupid on his bed of flowers,
Lov'd without knowing Love. Or if you think,
My fickle heart will scorn the baby-tale,
Describe some transport of our warmer passion.—
Paint the secluded bower where last we met,
While all the mild and blushing western sky,
Glow'd like the flame of Love's delightful torch,
And my fond heart, first, felt thy bosom beat.

LORENZO O Maddalen, my ever dear adored.

MADDALEN Horror! avaunt! this is thy father's hand.

ACT I, Scene III

LORENZO In what strange chaos do I find myself?
The film of flax is stronger in the flame,
Than all my resolutions in her presence.
Why stay I ling'ring and resolving still?
To me she cannot be unmarried; never!
Sure some fatality abhorred detains me;
Some devil plotting for my better part.

ACT I, Scene IV

VALDINI *and* LORENZO.

VALDINI Lorenzo! how is this? still sad, still thoughtful.
Since first I told you I had fixt to marry,
Your face has chang'd, and with a slighting eye
You oft, too pettishly, have heard and noted,
Those preparations, not extravagant,
Which our condition claims for such events.
And know you not the marriage is perform'd?

LORENZO I do, my Lord.

VALDINI Politeness might have taught,
At least, to feign a joy for the occasion.
I did expect a little more from you.
'Tis true I am your father.—

LORENZO O my Lord!

VALDINI And step-mother's are often bad enough;
But you are not a child; and, as I hope,
My wife has qualities that you may love.
I have inform'd you, that, in early youth,

My heart was pledg'd to Maddalena's mother,
But victims, at the shrine of family pride,
We both were sacrificed. I went, abroad,
Soon after my espousal of your mother;
Who, had she liv'd, might have redeem'd my heart.
She died in giving birth to you.

LORENZO My Lord!

VALDINI Her ample dowery, great beyond my wants,
With just economy for you I nursed;
And now I come to render my account,
With the full rights, estates, and moveables.
I ever held them but as family trusts,
Although they cost me all my youthful hopes.
Think not the offspring of a second bed,
Shall touch one title that to you belongs.

LORENZO O my good Lord! my truly noble father!
You know me not. Of small import to me,
Are these vile documents of ill-starr'd love.
Keep them, and with them all that they convey,
For some more happy progeny.

VALDINI My dear Lorenzo! you perplex me much.
What is this grief that presses down your mind?
'Tis not my marriage then that vexes you?
What mean you? speak?

LORENZO 'Tis now, alas, too late!

ACT I, Scene V

DUTCHESS *and* VALDINI.

DUTCHESS Joy! joy, my Lord! how does my Lady niece?
But why alone? True lovers, fresh like you,

Should be at other sport. Tut, musty parchments!
Go; go and rustle silks. Where's my sweetheart?

VALDINI Whom?

DUTCHESS Don Lorenzo, my dear nephew now.
O! how I long to tease the snappish dog,
He used to turn on me so snarling.

VALDINI Why?

DUTCHESS I took such pleasure to disturb his wooing.

VALDINI Wooing!

DUTCHESS Desperate wooing. O he was mad!
Mad as Leander, who across the sea
Swam every night, while Ero, cunning toad,
Stood at th' uncurtain'd window with a light,
His polar star, the pharos of his port![5]
But love, sweet love, makes conjurors of all.

VALDINI I never heard of Don Lorenzo's passion!

DUTCHESS No! How delightful! but the Duke is here;
And he has grown so stern and sour of late,
That I am scarcely free to breathe with him.
I'll to the bride and feel her palpitations.

ACT I, Scene VI

DUKE *and* VALDINI.

DUKE Bridegroom?

VALDINI Well!

---

5 A pharos is a lighthouse, the most famous being that formerly at Alexandria.

DUKE Grave! with solemn parchments too!
Strange occupation for your wedding-day.—
My prattling Dutchess has been teasing?

VALDINI No.
Her Grace is gaily hearted, and delights
To catch the flying pleasures as they pass.
But she has told me news.

DUKE I hope not bad?

VALDINI Not, certainly, as she appears to think.
Has e'er your Grace heard of Lorenzo's passion?

DUKE Passion, my Lord! what passion?

VALDINI Love.

DUKE For whom?

VALDINI As yet I have not heard, but much I fear—

DUKE 'Tis a conceit of her's—give it no heed.

VALDINI But I have seen my son thoughtful and sad.

DUKE (*Fool that I was, not to prepare for this.*)

VALDINI My Lord?

DUKE My Lord?

VALDINI I thought your Grace had spoken.

DUKE I said it must be some slight flame. With whom?

VALDINI I, rather, fear 'tis an unworthy charm,

Something his reason blushes to disclose.
And yet he is not one of that complexion.
I know him—just, high-minded and topful
Of noble magnanimity—all that
Becomes his birth and splendid expectation.

DUKE Such often err a little from the straight.

VALDINI True! but the errant ever show some glimpse
Of livelier spirit than Lorenzo bears.
A mild, a temperate virtue, meek but firm,
Pervades his gen'rous nature. I am vext,
And will to-morrow question him myself.

DUKE My wife was gossiping to tell you this.

VALDINI Not so, my Lord; 'twas in her sprightly way,
And but for something, troubled and distress'd,
Which I had noticed in Lorenzo's mind,
I should have, lightly, pass'd her Grace's wit.—
He has refused to take his mother's dower.

DUKE How?

VALDINI He has.

DUKE You then have offer'd it?

VALDINI All.

DUKE Money and Estates?

VALDINI Yes: all I possess'd.

DUKE How meant you then to keep your own degree?

VALDINI My pensions, recompence of faithful service,

And the small relic that has still been spared,
By a long line of wasteful prodigals,
Make yet enough for a philosopher.

DUKE But for my niece?[6]

VALDINI My wife, I trust, will learn
On better ground to build her happiness,
Than fleeting wealth affords. Your Grace knows well,
How slight a tenure, in this changeful age,
We hold for all that makes us what we are.

DUKE She had been better with your son.

VALDINI My Lord!—
To-day, from you, I can take no offence.
If wealth was all her aim—Lorenzo's wealth,
Doubtless, surpasses mine an hundred fold.

DUKE He too is young, her match in years.

VALDINI Well, well,
Let all that pass, the marriage now is o'er.
Your pardon, 'till I put these papers by.

ACT I, Scene VII

DUKE.

What have I done? Who could have fancied this?
I thought the Count had been a man of sense!
To live so long in the great world of courts;
To deal and traffic with the bought and sold,
And ever too with most renown'd success;
And yet to talk like a romantic youth!—
A very boy o'er his poetic scrawls,

---

6 The original has "neice."

Could not have feign'd a wilder flight than this.
O! how have I been so beside myself?
To trust this fool of nature, and to give
Him due and credence for the fame he bears:
A fame obtain'd by fortune's accidents!—
Dolt that I was, not to suspect his weakness.
And I have sacrificed poor Maddalen!

ACT I, Scene VIII

DUTCHESS *and* DUKE.

DUTCHESS Fine work! fine work! a merry wedding-day!
The bridegroom here, with parchments in his hand,[7]
Majestically grave: the bride, forlorn,
There, with a handkerchief dejected sits,
Wiping away her final virgin tears.
Were she in process of a lewd divorce,
Caught in the fact, she could not sob it more.

DUKE Your silly meddling and unruly tongue,
Is ever breeding trouble. What is this,
That you have loosely chattered to the Count?

DUTCHESS O! to be sure, all that mishaps is mine!
I put the odious parchments in his hand,
I put the dismal handkerchief in hers.[8]

DUKE Woman! no more of this! Hear my firm will.
Never again speak you that e'er between
The Countess and her son, Lorenzo. Mark!

DUTCHESS Her son!

DUKE Ought pass'd but such as freely may,

---

7 The original has "bridgroom."
8 The original has "her's."

In mixt assembly, pass with laugh and freak
Of youthful gaiety. Mind nothing more.

DUTCHESS O heart of me! I always thought no good
Could come of their nocturnal whisperings.
But lovers will be lovers, certain sure.

DUKE There is more hazard in your giddy head,
Than in your foolish tongue.

DUTCHESS Good words my Lord.
I'll be as silent as your ancestors,
Ay, where they sit upon their monuments,
In what concerns the honour of our house.—
I'll to her instantly and tax her with 't.

DUKE Heav'ns and earth! the woman is possess'd!
But here Lorenzo comes, let us be calm.

DUTCHESS In truth, a handsome portly youth to see;
A pleasant vision to a lady's eye.

ACT I, Scene IX

LORENZO, DUKE, *and* DUTCHESS.

LORENZO I thought the Count, my father, had been here.

DUKE He just has stepp'd into his closet. Well!
And so, Lorenzo, you refuse to take
Your mother's princely dower?

DUTCHESS Have I my ears?

LORENZO Doubtless, my Lord, 'tis much to your content.

DUKE Could I have but divined the Count's—[9]

---

[9] The original has "devined."

LORENZO No more!
No more of that! What is done, is.—

DUTCHESS Poor youth!

LORENZO The fortune all shall yet be Maddalen's—
Her children yet shall have their mother's price.

DUTCHESS Hark ye! some one of them may be your own.

LORENZO Ha! what malignant fiend predicts to thee?

ACT I, Scene X

DUKE *and* LORENZO.

DUKE What said the Dutchess?

LORENZO Wretch!

DUKE How now? What's this?

LORENZO Yes, sordid wretch! Curs'd trafficker in hearts,
When thou art damn'd, be it thy punishment
To writhe in molten gold.

DUKE Sure he is mad!

LORENZO Had I but told my father, trusted him,
His noble nature would have sav'd us all.
O fatal diffidence! O deadly doubt!
O hesitation that decides too late!

DUKE I can no longer, sir! brook this contempt.

LORENZO Contempt! no; abhorrence, triple accurs'd!
The loathsome toad, with its foul speckled breast,

Is less detestable than thou art, wretch!
With thy crime-spotted soul.

DUKE Draw, draw, I say!

LORENZO Would'st thou to hell so soon?

DUKE Draw, villain! draw!

LORENZO Villain from thee!—Villain! put up thy sword.

DUKE I will, I will.

LORENZO Ay do: go use thy purse.

ACT I, Scene XI

LORENZO.

Here I am not myself: each petty word
That bears allusion to my former state,
Like the small spark that fires a magazine,
With terrible combustion fills my breast.—
To-morrow—yes, to-morrow, I will go.
But if so soon, what will my father think?
And yet, he must not know the painful cause.
The sacrifice is made! Then let not me,
By wild temerity, make worse the ill.
No: but the rather, all that in me lies,
Use for a happier aim—again the Dutchess.

ACT I, Scene XII

DUTCHESS *and* LORENZO.

DUTCHESS Lorenzo! is the Duke gone hence, Lorenzo?

LORENZO Yes. Well?

DUTCHESS Come, come, we shall be friends again.

LORENZO (*A garrulous good-hearted soul.*) We shall.—
Pardon my fury.

DUTCHESS Never speak of it.
Between ourselves, the Duke's a—I know what.
He is so gruff and turkish in his way,
By Mary, Virgin, I am more his slave
Than his true Dutchess, wedded by the hand.
'Tis all his doing, this dull wedding-day.

LORENZO Most true it is.

DUTCHESS No joke, no revelry.
I might, as well, have come in weeds of woe,
As in my jewels, and this gay brockade,
Bought purposely. See this delightful flounce!
My own device! No respite, day nor night,
I gave th' embroid'rer till it was complete.
Behold what it has come to! Heaven look to't!
But solemn visages and wat'ry eyes,
Are dismal omens on a wedding-day.
And lo! the bride, dull as the moon eclips'd.

ACT I, Scene XIII

MADDALEN *and* DUTCHESS.

MADDALEN Your grace alone!

DUTCHESS No: here!—Why, what is this?
As I have soul in me, the world's depraved;
All courtesy and gentle manners gone,
And weddings held as sad obsequies.
Here was I standing, as I thought I was;
Holding a chat in pleasant negligence
With Don Lorenzo. But, he, like a ghost,

A vapoury ghost, has vanish'd into air.—
Well! by my troth, I have good cause to fret.
Snubb'd and brow-beaten when I would make mirth,—
As little heeded as a cuckoo clock.
I may, as well, at once, go say my prayers.

MADDALEN Truly, dear aunt, all inauspicious lowers.
In vain, in vain, I would my heart control,[10]
But still some dire tempestuous thought succeeds,
And whirls me to despair.

DUTCHESS It is not wise
To think so much, now that your knell is rung.

MADDALEN O hopeless me! it was, indeed, my knell.

DUTCHESS Go to, go to.—Catch not my words so sadly.
You're not the first, as I could tell myself,
That has been worried from her own true love.
But thank your stars, since they would have it so,
That you have got a husband, gracious, noble;
A man, who, but to say the least of him,
Is worth ten thousand dukes; and then his son—

MADDALEN Ah! name him not, let me forget him now.
O idle wish, that only serves to bring
His darling image warmer to my heart.

DUTCHESS Fye! These obstrep'rous fits become you ill.
He was your lover: dangled here and there,
Made piteous sonnets to your smiles and tears;
Danc'd with you, laugh'd with you, and if 'twere known,
Perhaps, a score or two of kisses stole.
The world is old, and such things are not new:
Come, pass them by, and think of other cheer.—
I have got news that will content your heart.

---

10 The original has "controul."

MADDALEN Alas, to me, all tidings are alike.
My part and int'rest in this world is done.

DUTCHESS Lorenzo—

MADDALEN Dearest, ever worshipp'd, name,
Be thou the word of courage to my soul,
In the great enterprize that I have sworn.

DUTCHESS Tut, tut, niece! you displease me much.—No more.
You know his mother's wealth and large estates,
Without restraint, were to his father given.

MADDALEN For them, I know that I was sold and doomed.

DUTCHESS Well! who could think, what the good count has done?
Resign'd them all to him!

MADDALEN What! to Lorenzo?

DUTCHESS All!

MADDALEN Just, noble, father! Now what says the duke?
What says the bargainer? My brain is fired.

DUTCHESS But not one florin will Lorenzo touch,
So all is safe. What means this hideous laugh?
Heav'ns! are ye sane? Why do ye glare at me?
O! I am terrified.—Niece! Maddalen!
O my sweet Maddalen! help!—

MADDALEN Hush! there's none.

ACT II, Scene I

VALDINI *and* LORENZO.

VALDINI I ask no more; convinc'd that this decision,
Springs from just cause for manly resolution;

That prudence also dictates to conceal.
But when do you depart?

LORENZO To-morrow.

VALDINI How!
So soon! to-morrow?

LORENZO Speedily, I mean.
I should say, rather, in a day or two.

VALDINI Lorenzo! Is there danger in delay?

LORENZO My lord!

VALDINI Reserve: I cannot then approve,
When evil falls, and you see all its scope,
Trust to the native courage of your breast,
And such auxiliar aid as chance may send[11]
To master the misfortune: trust yourself,
And trust your destiny; for such begets,
That self possession which endures the shock
Of rough adversity, and lifts the man
Above the waves and currents of the time.
But when the matter hangs in dread, and may,
By strength or enterprize, be yet repell'd,
Then call your friends, take counsel, and take aid.

LORENZO But when the fear in our own frailty lies?

VALDINI (*'Tis so.*)

LORENZO (*What have I said? he seems disturb'd.*)

VALDINI The dutchess told me, in her merry way,
That you have been in love.

LORENZO My lord! my lord!

---

11 Galt may have dropped the final vowel of "auxiliary" for reasons of meter.

VALDINI Be not alarm'd: why, there is nothing in't.
A thing most natural. But love is blind,[12]
And leads his votaries, oft, far from virtue.
You now repent your passion?

LORENZO Pity me.

VALDINI 'Twas then unworthy you? Her grace, I think,
Told me as much.

LORENZO (*He knows but half the truth.*)
No, no, my lord; 'twas a most worthy love:
Youth, beauty, virtue, and illustrious birth;
All that could charm the heart and eye of youth,
And claim the favour of sedater age.

VALDINI But you were not approv'd?

LORENZO Approv'd! alas!
O! with such ardour.—

VALDINI Then why hid from me?
Who is the lady?

LORENZO Seek to know no more,
For she is married.

VALDINI Now, I am content.
Enough; go when you will. But some one comes.
The duke!

LORENZO Let me retire?

VALDINI O poor Lorenzo!

---

12 The phrase "love is blind" was first found in Chaucer's *Merchant's Tale* (c.1405), and later in Shakespeare's *Two Gentlemen of Verona*, *Henry V*, and *The Merchant of Venice*.

ACT II, Scene II

DUKE *and* VALDINI.

DUKE Your brow is somewhat clear'd. The morning cloud
Has vanish'd, and your face begins to show
The solar aspect of a blithe bridegroom.

VALDINI My heart is eas'd. Lorenzo has been here,
And so disclosed the secret of his gloom,
That I am prouder still of such a son.
Come, now we'll to the bride, nor keep the dutchess
In longer expectation of the cheer.

DUKE Softly, my lord; call your philosophy.
The heat to-day, and flurry in her thoughts,
The nat'ral offspring of her maiden fancies,
Have, who can sift these frailties from the fair?
Compell'd the bride to take some short repose.

VALDINI What! and not I inform'd!

DUKE O a mere trifle,
Count, women still are women, weaker vessels;
And we should lightly look upon their flaws.

VALDINI Is not a physician call'd?

DUKE Fye, my lord,
The dutchess and her maids are worth a college
In such a case.—What has Lorenzo said?

VALDINI He has confess'd all that I wish'd to know.

DUKE His passion! well, with whom is he in love?

VALDINI It was not fit, for me, to ask him more.

DUKE No!

VALDINI Certainly, for she is married.

DUKE What!

VALDINI It might, as I the matter understand,
Disturb the happiness, or taint the honour
Of some illustrious house; therefore, my son
Conceals it wisely. He has well resolv'd
To shun the danger, and to seek abroad,
In the variety of other lands,
Solace for his distressing heart-disease.

DUKE And when does he depart? Not soon, I hope?

VALDINI With all convenient speed—perhaps to-morrow.

DUKE I am amaz'd! So soon?

VALDINI Virtue resolv'd,
Can never act too soon. The countess here!

DUKE (*He goes abroad—patience, patience, revenge.*)

ACT II, Scene III

VALDINI, MADDALEN, *and* DUKE.

VALDINI You still seem pale, and deeply agitated.

MADDALEN O! my good lord, I cannot bear this long.

VALDINI Where is the dutchess? she is ill indeed.
A doctor instantly!

MADDALEN My uncle here!
Why does he go? stop him, my lord, stop! stop!

DUKE (*All, all will out: her brain is surely craz'd.*)

VALDINI This cumb'rous dress, oppresses you, I think.

MADDALEN Why did I ever put it on? Off! off!
Ye hateful vanities, ye load my head.
My wretched head will rest without your weight.

DUKE This is wild speech.

VALDINI My lord! what have you done?

DUKE What? I!

VALDINI This is a fever of the mind.

DUKE A doctor should be here.

MADDALEN O stop!

VALDINI My lord!

DUKE What mean you, count, by this impassion'd tone?
There is no danger.

VALDINI No!

DUKE (*Angels and Saints!*)

MADDALEN What has the duke done that you dare him so?

VALDINI What has he done?

DUKE (*She seems to check herself.*)

MADDALEN What has he done? for shame to ask so rudely,
When he has given me to be your wife.

'Tis true he never promised me your heart,
Nor could he promise mine to you.

VALDINI My lord!

MADDALEN The dutchess has been telling me a tale,—
A dismal tale, I never heard before,—
That the mild image smiling in yon picture,
Was my own mother.

DUKE A sad tale, ill-timed.

VALDINI I crave your grace a million, million pardons.

DUKE You did indeed confound me, count. The dutchess,
Still heedless, prattles, and must be endured.

VALDINI Ah my dear Maddalen, you have my heart;
And with it too, that fixt and firm esteem,
Which younger lovers seldom know to give.

DUKE He is your husband.

MADDALEN Had he been my father—

VALDINI Ah! why that sigh? I will be both to you,
Husband and father.

MADDALEN Horrible! horrible!

ACT II, Scene IV

DUKE.

How shall I from this labyrinth escape?
Ever unguarded, in some luckless hour
My wife may blab. And still, my honest care,

This love-sick damsel, like a maniac treats;
And raves of guilt and victims. On the edge,
The brink of shame I walk; yet I meant good.
No: I was not bound to tell the count—No—
That's clear and fair. And how knew I their love?
I was no confident. Rumour; report;
But never proof by eye nor ear, had I,—
Letter nor lay; not even foolish sonnet.
This I can swear; all this! but the count—well?—
The count may say, I should have told him. What?
Could I repeat to him my wife's conceit:
He could not think, that one of my repute
Would stoop to that. Yet, he may call it trick.
Trick! fraud! to study my own niece's good!
Po! sentimental stuff: he is a man,
And will not whine such poetry of passion.

ACT II, Scene V

DUKE *and* DUTCHESS.

DUKE Come here! hither, I say! O woman! woman!
What craz'd infernal meddles with thy brain?
The raven's bode and owlet's evil cry,
Are happier heraldings than thy jay-chatter.

DUTCHESS Your own mis-deeds, my lord, throw not on me.
I wash my hands; and pure at these my palms,
Is my poor conscience of this day's ill work.

DUKE What mean you? Ha! you turn'd accuser too?

DUTCHESS My lord, unhand me, or I'll raise the house.

DUKE Alas! alas! we have been man and wife,
Full thirty years; would you betray me now?

DUTCHESS My lord! my lord! you make me very sad.

DUKE I am bewitch'd—I am beside myself;
To take the thing in this outrageous sense,
And thus to sink before a silly—Ha!

ACT II, Scene VI

DUKE, LORENZO, *and* DUTCHESS.

DUKE (*Hell! hateful sight.*)

LORENZO Wonders will never cease!
What! has the duke been puling for his faults?
Or has he found in you such charms renew'd,
That he was aping lovers adoration?

DUTCHESS 'Twas frolic all—I so become this dress:
My youth seems so renew'd.

LORENZO No fibs, good aunt.

DUKE She's like the eagles, Don Lorenzo.

LORENZO What! Does she too prey on the innocent lambs?
(*Now the poison searches.*)

DUTCHESS Gentle, Lorenzo.
What a day is this?

LORENZO It is a wedding-day!
A wedding-day! Come, my lord duke, look blithe.
What! uncle, uncle, uncle, ho! come laugh?
Give us the cheer, give us the wedding-joy,
You made the feast. Ah, bungling cook,
To leave out all the joy.

DUTCHESS (*He too is touch'd.*)

DUKE Softly, Lorenzo. O! in pity spare—

LORENZO And has it come to this? Drink thy own chalice.
Such pity as was shown to me and mine,
Thou greedy dotard, I will show to thee.
When two young hearts lay bleeding at your feet,
How did you spurn and tread upon their pain?
But now, when heav'n's red hand of fire is forth,
Opening to seize and dash thee to thy doom,
Think'st thou that I should spare? Should justice mar?

DUKE Who feels no pity, yet remorse may sting.

LORENZO What do I hear? audacious driv'ler, hence.

DUTCHESS He is not made of stone; in love forbear!

LORENZO Love! Love it is that nerves me to this pitch;
Loves barbs my taunts, goads me to wring his heart.

DUKE Opprobrious boy! what knew I of your love?[13]

LORENZO Does the cur turn?

DUKE Where is the proof?
Where is the evidence? produce! produce!
See, here I stand, ready to meet your charge.

LORENZO What juggling devil, tempts my quicken'd sword?
Let me look at thee? poor old man!—begone.

ACT II, Scene VII

DUTCHESS *and* LORENZO.

DUTCHESS Oh! my full heart will burst.—Fye on you, fye!
Who could have thought that one so mild as you,

---

13 The original has "approbrious" and the Errata suggestion that this be read as "opprobrious" has been followed here.

As soft in manners, as the silky fur
Upon the bosom of a playing kitten,
Could have been like a raging tyger fierce?
The tyger dam robb'd of her helpless young,
Is less tempestuous. Out on you; shame!—
But woe and sorrow, never to be cured,
Can come of these deliriums. Fye! Lorenzo.

LORENZO 'Tis the last time. Now he has felt the scorch;
My rage shall flame no more. Deep in my breast
The low unquenchable consuming fire
Of my peculiar grief, forever hid,
Shall ne'er again molest. I leave him now,
To the rous'd scorpions of his own regrets.

ACT II, Scene VIII

DUTCHESS.

Sure, sure no good can come of plots and plans,
That a weak woman's simple jointless talk,
So often brings to jeopardy.
I cannot speak, but flash and there's a storm;—
Live silent; or but to say, yea or nay,—
I may as well go lay me down to die.
I'm a repeater, by my maker made;
And when I'm press'd, must tell how the time goes.
But I can stay at home—lie on a shelf—
See no one—nothing hear—sit like an abbess;
I may as well, with hood and veil, at once,
Go serve my God; and for this sprightly fan,
Sigh to a fly-benastyed crucifix.
Was it for this, that I was made a dutchess?

ACT II, Scene IX[14]

VALDINI *and* DUTCHESS.

VALDINI The countess, more composed, requests your grace.—

DUTCHESS I'm going home, She's now a wedded wife,
And on her own discretion must depend.
She was a babe; a sprawling, squalling babe,
When she was given to these arms of mine:
I cherish'd her, I bred her from the bud,
Till she was all the rose that you have seen.

VALDINI What has eclips'd your grace's gaiety?

DUTCHESS She was the pride and apple of my eye;
And all my hope and wish'd for recompence,
Was to behold her happy wedding-day;
And be to some sweet imp of her's again,
What I had been to her. But what has chanced!

VALDINI It may be as you wish'd.

DUTCHESS[15] My heart was high,
And all the court and town knew how it beat:
There's not a mill'ners wench that has not heard.
O! I shall be the trading stock of scandal,
For thrice nine days, and more.

VALDINI Patience, be calm.

DUTCHESS I won't be patient. How, my lord, can you
Bear all this too, nor grudge along with me?
Me-thinks you have good cause.

---
14 The original has "Scene V" and the Errata suggestion that this be read as "Scene IX" has been followed here.
15 The original has "Ducthess".

VALDINI 'Twas accident;
And 'twould have been as well, had it so pleas'd
Your grace to-day, not to have troubled her;
I would myself, have ta'en a fitter time
And told her all.

DUTCHESS Who could foresee
That, rapt'rous as a nymph poetical,
She would have rav'd about her mother's doom;
And with such heart-affecting wail exclaim'd,
That she, herself, was your predestin'd daughter.

VALDINI It had been better, had she known it sooner.

DUTCHESS There you say truth; but such, forsooth, is rank.
Our dignites, the honours of our blood,[16]
Claim these concealments. Taints, sins, and divorces!
All must be stored to break our hearts at last.

VALDINI Alas! too true—your words have wisdom's weight.

DUTCHESS Had it pleased Heav'n t've made me but the dame
Of some blithe burgher, round and sound at heart,
Whom I, at will, might have ta'en by the arm,
And gone well-welcomed to our joking neighbours;
I had been happier than with all this pomp,
Titles, and carriages—begraced vexations.
But madam comes.

ACT II, Scene X

VALDINI, MADDALEN, *and* DUTCHESS.

VALDINI Come in the turn of time.
Her grace is here offended, much incensed,
And you must pacify.

---

16 The original has "dignites".

MADDALEN Oh! how unfit.
There is a full and thick'ning sadness here,
That nothing earthly can remove.

DUTCHESS There now!
At it again!

MADDALEN Pity, and chide me not.
In vain, in vain I strive to check my grief.
The fatal courage that sustained me through
The deathful ceremony, is no more.

VALDINI (*Oh! oh! this sorrow is not new.*)

MADDALEN My lord!

VALDINI A sudden pang across my temples shot.

MADDALEN Heav'n help us all!

DUTCHESS Amen! may well say I!

VALDINI 'Tis past— 'twas momentary—let's be gay.

DUTCHESS My heart is changed—I have no mind for mirth.
I could in some sad corner sit and cry.

VALDINI Where is the duke? Why, what dejects your grace?
Where is the duke, I say? O! Maddalen,
Why look you on me so amaz'd?

MADDALEN My lord!

VALDINI Well. Speak!

MADDALEN Call no one here!

DUTCHESS She frightens me.

MADDALEN Hear and record, ye regist'rers of heaven.
To-day, I at the sacred altar knelt,
A virgin pure, and took the marriage vow,
To be to this high-honoured, virtuous man,
A faithful wife. Again, I take the oath,—
While in my heart revolves the tide of life;
While sense can act and minister to thought,
I will, even to the syllable, perform
All my tremendous vow. Why call the duke?

VALDINI Alas! you, in this awful act, but show
What I should ne'er have known, or known before.

DUTCHESS I'll to a nunnery, this very night.

MADDALEN Ha! where was I, not to have thought of that,
Before my fatal vows.

VALDINI Within? help, help!

ACT II, Scene XI

VALDINI, DUTCHESS, LORENZO *and* MADDALEN.

LORENZO Now she revives.

DUTCHESS O my sweet Maddalen!
'Tis I, your poor old aunt—know you me not?
Off cursed glitter, wrap of misery.
Oh! better in a ragged blanket, driv'n
From titled thresholds, weeping for a crumb,
Than to have known what I have known to-day.
What would you here, Lorenzo?

MADDALEN Gentle vision!

LORENZO O Maddalen! my lovely Maddalen!

MADDALEN I am thy mother, boy.

VALDINI It is Lorenzo!

ACT III, Scene I

DUKE.

He has departed; but the ruffians staunch
Will hound his track, before the setting sun
Has turn'd the mountain shadows from the vale,
And will be posted in the olive wood:
There let him bloody lie, gash'd to the heart.—
He'd do as much for me. What had I done,
To be so stabb'd by scorn; and like one curs'd,
Shook o'er the crater of the fiery deep,
And scourg'd with execrations? Do I not,
By this revenge, draw on the taunted doom?
For him, I may have over-reach'd myself,
And cast my own eternal gem away!

ACT III, Scene II

VALDINI *and* DUKE.

VALDINI Where is my son? Where has Lorenzo gone?

DUKE (*Then it is done. He cannot me suspect.*)

VALDINI What! dumb? Why do you press your downward face
So with your clenched hand, and hang so shrunk,
Crampt on the start? Sure there is guilt in thee!—
And this dire marriage was compell'd and forc'd
In the full knowledge of Lorenzo's passion!
Answer me?

DUKE Yes: no.

VALDINI Yes! no!

DUKE (*'Tis not so.*)

VALDINI What is not so? Cannot your grace reply?

DUKE (*It is not as I fear'd.*) I'm better now.

VALDINI Old man, old man, retire to thy confessor.
All is too plain. I ask to learn no more!
Whither so fast?

DUKE To ride; to breathe the air.

VALDINI May Heav'n thy strange-timed errand speed.

DUKE Amen!

ACT III, Scene III

VALDINI.

Is there no cure? Are oaths of such firm knot,
That nothing human ever may untie?
What is an oath? A bond, a pact with God;
In which the rights to our celestial part,
Are lodged, in pawn with the eternal foe;
Never to be redeem'd, but by the just
Fulfilment of the bond—the dreadful bond!
But, may not Heav'n cancel and set us free;
And by the trumpet sounding from the cloud
Of threat'ning woe, command us from the path
Of our sworn pilgrimage, to shun the storm?—
Of this, who dare be judge?

ACT III, Scene IV

VALDINI *and* DUTCHESS.

VALDINI What means your grace, by this funereal garb?—
We need no outward pageants to our grief.

DUTCHESS The ominous and fatal black of woe,
Suits best the day and my dejected heart.
All is awry, and sorrow comes to all.
Sure some malignant planet rules the sky,
And sheds distress and madness on the earth.
I met the duke, as he prepared to mount,—
The foot in stirrup, and the main in hand:
I said, 'God help him,' piously, and pass'd.
When fierce as any chain-broke bedlamite,[17]
He rush'd upon me; shook me by the throat;
Call'd me a witch, to wear these weeds of death;
And flung me from him, as a thing most vile.
Then to his horse, and ere I found myself,
Was through the portal like a peal of thunder.
Where is he gone, my lord?

VALDINI I think not of him.
Go where he will, he cannot harm me more.
Oh! he has spill'd to me, the joy of life,
And broke the cup. My poor Lorenzo too!
And Maddalen! all share the self same doom.
With what fell mineral is that man compounded?
Who, to the altar of the golden Moloch,
Can, smiling, see, the helpless victims bound!

DUTCHESS I wish that I were dead, and on my bier;
Borne in the hearse, with all vain heraldry
And chanting friars, to the mouldly vault;
There to remain with grinning sculls alone,

---

17 Asylum of Bethlehem (Bedlam) in Lambeth, London.

'Till I shall hear the angel in the air,
And rise, to be a cherub of the sky,
With my sweet Maddalen; far, far above
The bearded tyrants of this wicked world.

VALDINI If simple worth, a bosom without gall,
And childlike innocence retain'd to age,
Procure admission to the home of faith;
Full many a proud and wordly wise afar,[18]
Shall gaze, astonish'd at thy bright ascending.
What noise is that? a tumult fills the court!

DUTCHESS Heav'n be with us!

ACT III, Scene V

DUTCHESS, LORENZO, *and* VALDINI.

DUTCHESS Ha! Lorenzo bloody!

LORENZO My lord, I think, it is, it is, not mortal.—
I have been way-laid, but not to be robb'd.
The gang struck at my life.

VALDINI Here, set him down—
Now is the dreadful curtain torn from all;
Hie to the guard—help! help! call up the house.
Retire, retire; quit this terrific scene,
Ill-fated dame! He sinks, he falls, he dies.
Oh my Lorenzo! Now he breathes again.

ACT III, Scene VI

MADDALEN, VALDINI, *and* LORENZO.

MADDALEN What wretch art thou, that with such outcry, fills
This trembling house; marring the magic dreams

---

18 "wordly" most likely meant to be "worldly".

Of my sweet med'cin'd sleep? Lorenzo! what!
Hast thou been at it, and would be before me?
Perfidious rogue! that could thy true love leave.
I'll pinch thy cheeks for this. We'll go together,
Though never, never to be man and wife,
We yet can faithful die; lie in one grave;
And free from incest, mingle dust with dust.

LORENZO My lord, take her away; her thoughts are wild.

MADDALEN Forbear! forbear! this should have been Lorenzo's.
As I have sworn love! it cannot be thine.
Oh! my good lord, my husband! priest-made husband.—
What is't that I would say?

VALDINI Ill-fated fair.
Come, gentle! let me lead thee to thy room?

MADDALEN Oh! fye bridegroom; look at that dying man!
To think of bedding, in the teeth of death.
Fye, fye, fye, fye.

LORENZO Oh! let me have some drink.

VALDINI Attendants! Water!—Rise sweet Maddalen,
Rise from thy knees, nor gaze upon him so.

MADDALEN What metamorphosis is working here?
My lov'd Lorenzo, once so fresh and fair,
Is vanishing away; and in his stead,
A pale and glazy-eyed cadavre grows.

ACT III, Scene VII

DUTCHESS, MADDALEN, VALDINI, *and* LORENZO.

DUTCHESS I must come here. The chamber of grim death
Is not so fearful as the specter'd fancies,

That rise among my thoughts. The horses hoofs,
Ringing upon the pavement of the court,
Clank in my ears, like the black gibbet's chain;
And e'en the silly creaking of a door,
Sounds like the swinging of a murd'rer's bones.

MADDALEN Ha! my kind aunt; come here, come here, come here.
Hush, hush,—there's am elopement going on.
Marriages are made in heav'n. We'll go there.
In black! coffins and charnal vaults! dear aunt,
What prompting spirit put you up to this?
Lorenzo! look! her grace is ready for us.

VALDINI How feel you now, Lorenzo?

LORENZO Better, better.—
Think you it was the duke that set them on?

VALDINI We'll see to it hereafter.

LORENZO Was it not strange,
If they were robbers, first to think of murder?

VALDINI Most strange! but 'tis a day of prodigies!

DUTCHESS Oh! my dear Maddalen, pray thee, forbear.
Thy thoughts are like the yellow falling leaves,
That wildly rustle in the ev'ning gale,
Dispers'd afar. Rude was the wintry blast,
That so untimely smote my blooming tree.
I thought to sit beneath the lovely shade,
'Tending young lambs, all in the setting sun:
But now, it waves a wild phantastic head,
And soon will lie, before the feller, low.
Oh! turn from me, these pale heart-breaking eyes?
Look at thy lover, bleeding on the floor.

MADDALEN Cheat me no more! Know I not my Lorenzo?
Was't not enough to foist the old one on me?
Think you, I always will submit to this;
And take for him, that potsherd of a man?
I hate the sight. By Cupid's dimpled smiles,
The ghastly mimic apes Lorenzo's beauty.

ACT III, Scene VIII

DUKE, VALDINI, MADDALEN, LORENZO, *and* DUTCHESS.

DUKE My friend, my friend, what dire mischance is this?
Our morning's error, time might have retrieved;
Some other, fairer, won again his heart;
And Cupid, with a rosy garland, bound
The lion of your rage.

VALDINI Guards! seize the duke.

DUKE How now, my lord!

VALDINI Hence! hollow-sounding brass,
The lion claims his prey.—Bear him to jail.

DUTCHESS Forbear, Forbear.

MADDALEN Where am I? What are these?
Did not the doctor give me medicine?
I saw the count, the label'd phial pour,
And serve the draught as I lay in my bed.—
How came I here? Or, am I in a dream,
And these but visions, metaphysical,
Bred in my drugged sleep? This feels of stuff,
My lord, your grace. They are corporeal too!
To touch, as palpable as to the sight.
But why the dutchess in these weeds of woe,
The floor all bloody, and Lorenzo pale;

And wherefore hold these felon-guards, the duke?
My lord; I was, to-day, married to you!

VALDINI Alas! it has been so.

MADDALEN Explain me this?

LORENZO (*Her reason brightens from the opiates fume,*
And she may know me yet, before I die.)

VALDINI Her black, was but a strange forerunning fancy.
Lorenzo has been murderously stabb'd;
And I suspect the duke. Take him away!

MADDALEN Yet, yet, my lord, let him remain.

DUTCHESS What would she?

MADDALEN I now begin to feel myself again.
Lorenzo! how art thou? Courage, my love;
All goes right well. The duke shall have his due.
My lord, I'll be to you a faithful wife.
Stay, my Lorenzo! gentle spirit, stay.

ACT III, Scene IX

DUKE, VALDINI, DUTCHESS, *and* LORENZO.

DUKE You shall repent this gross indignity!
To charge a man of my exalted rank,
With such opprobrious crime. Let him there, speak,[19]
And charge me if he dare?

VALDINI You shall have justice.
'Twould not be well for men of our degree,

---

19 The original has "approbrious" and the Errata suggestion that this be read as "opprobrious" has been followed here.

The sires and guardians of the public law,
To higgle at the forefeit of such deeds.
Your grace knew well, when you set on this work,
What the great volumes of our country says.
The whisper'd conference; the jingled bribe;
The richer promise partially revealed;
And more temptations in the darken'd rear,
To bend the bloody panders to your will;
Were witness that you knew.

DUTCHESS O my good lord!
Let grey-hair'd pity plead for him and me?
Heav'n, by old age, has serv'd its warrant on him,
And soon the stern and grisly jailor, Death,
Must lead him to the bar. What better judge
Would you, my lord, for this great guilt, desire,
Than he that, with a white and shining hand,
Unlocks the clasps upon the book of life,
And reads the doom of all—of all the world?

LORENZO Pardon, my lord, my father, let him fly.

VALDINI My noble boy, Oh! my Lorenzo dies.

LORENZO Oh! where is Maddalen?

VALDINI Where is she gone?
Is there no help? Has yet no surgeon come?

LORENZO 'Twere all in vain. Let no one now approach.
My light burns dim, for all the oil is out.

DUKE Ill-fated victim! pardon me thy blood?

LORENZO Raise him, my lord. I bear no malice hence.
 Dutchess Come, rise? and let us stand apart and weep.
To mourn is all we have to do in life.

LORENZO Oh! where is Maddalen? Oh, but once more.—

VALDINI She comes, she comes! The guards may now withdraw.

ACT III, Scene X

MADDALEN, VALDINI, LORENZO, DUKE *and* DUTCHESS.

MADDALEN Ha! is he gone?

VALDINI No, Maddalen,—come here;
Support his head; it best becomes thy arm.

LORENZO Thanks, gentle father.

MADDALEN Sweet! how art thou now?
Methinks the ray has parted from his eye.
He breathes no more. Lorenzo is away!

VALDINI Rise, Maddalen; all now is past. What was
My boy, is—

DUKE Have I eyes, and see him weep?

DUTCHESS What is't that she is taking from her breast?
Help! help! horror! horror!

DUKE (*A double murder's mine!*)

VALDINI O thou tremendous source of destiny!
Restrain the devil madding in my bosom.
Guards! guards within! your duty now perform.

DUKE I ask not now to live. Honour and fame,
Ye tempt no more: titles and dignities,
Ye mixt the posset, share the surfeit too.

VALDINI O wretched fair! had we not blood enough!
Thou should'st have liv'd a sacred virgin wife,

And never pleasure would I had with thee,
But to bewail thy hapless lover's fate.

MADDALEN A little nearer yet Lorenzo's side,
My noble wedded lord! All I could give,
Honour, esteem, that loving of the mind,
Which earthly natures bear for higher beings,
Thy virtues had: the heart, the woman's love
Was bred and twined with his that's silent here.
Lay us together, where you wish to lie;
And when the all-confusing hand of time
Has done its part, may never herb nor flower,
Spring from the barren and abortive spot.
Come, my lord duke! look on your punishment.
But life is ebbing, and the last low sands
Are filt'ring in the glass. My gentle aunt,
Give me your hand to kiss. We little thought,
When I, beneath your fond maternal wing,
Cower'd from the churl, to take farewell like this.
Lorenzo! O Lorenzo! now we meet.
Lucre nor priest shall never part us more.
We go, dear shade, where no division's known,
Nor other boundary than light and love.

DUTCHESS 'Twas thus her mother died.

VALDINI Come, come away.

DUTCHESS Oh! let me look upon her once again?
Oh! Maddalen, that never more can smile;
I took thee from thy dying mother's breast,
A little baby, and to me you clung,—
My heart was full, and I could only weep.
Now thou art gone, and left me in thy stead,
A bloody piece of lifeless church-yard clay.
DUKE Guards! to the prison! Bear me to the jail.
DUTCHESS I will go with thee too;—sit in thy cell,
And think of Maddalen; but never speak.

I'll take thy old grey head upon my lap;
And when thou art asleep, I'll drop a tear;
But, it will be for my sweet Maddalen.
Amidst the tolling of the fatal bell,
I'll join the psalm, but think of Maddalen:
And when I see the axe gleam in the air,
I'll close my eyes and go to Maddalen.

DUKE Give me thy hand.

DUTCHESS Farewell.

DUKE Oh, my lord.

VALDINI Stop!
'Tis meet that I should well consider this.
Thy age, thy dignity, thy gentle wife,
Put in petition and entreat respite.—
My own particular wrongs I set aside;
And you, ye victims, that lie silent here,
What will the sacrifice avail to you?
For you and for myself, Revenge is mute;
But claims, with more than all the Grecian's art,
Atonement for the direful public crime.
His age! Age should have taught him as it came,
That retribution sternly follows crime.
The young in years, may for their errors plead,
Impetuous blood, and reason's twilight dim.
Years bear against him, and his dignity,
Still feebler pleads; for in our titled sphere
Of sordid metal, is the marriage ring.
Now comes humanity to tug my heart;
But, 'tis humanity that brings the charge.
Guards, do your duty! let the law prevail.

END.

AGAMEMNON, A Tragedy

Characters.

AGAMEMNON
EGYSTHUS

CLYTEMNESTRA
ARSINOE

The stage represents the vestibule of a palace.

ACT I, Scene I

CLYTEMNESTRA.

And Agamemnon will be here to-day!
Triumphant and adorn'd with trojan spoil.—
After ten years of danger, to survive!
What will become of me? O fatal hour,
In which I yielded to my slave, Egysthus:
Had I but held him still in his degree,
Nor with such blazon of my favour, shown

A doting heart to all the crowd of Argos.—
Some courtly sycophant, that woos promotion,
Will blab against us. O deluded victim,
So in the fume and riot of my passion,
To dare destruction. We cannot escape!

ACT I, Scene II

CLYTEMNESTRA *and* ARSINOE.

CLYTEMNESTRA The king returns to-day.

ARSINOE So I have heard.

CLYTEMNESTRA Why are you sad, Arsinoe? The news
Should meet, from you, a blithe and cheerful welcome.

ARSINOE But, what a welcome shall the king receive?
What honest hail will cheer his coming home?
Who will rejoice, when he recounts the war?
Who will not weep, when he describes his wounds,
And sigh with sorrow, that they were not mortal.

CLYTEMNESTRA Nurse, you grow bold.

ARSINOE Oh! well-a-day, that I
Have liv'd to see the royal babe I cherish'd,
When grown to manhood, and a hero fam'd,
Supplanted in his love, by a vile slave;—
A coarse, rank-smelling groom; a neighing groom;
But fit companion for the horse he tended.

CLYTEMNESTRA Forget you, woman, that I am the queen?

ARSINOE Oh! that the queen had ne'er forgot herself:
And where, Oh where is Agamemnon's child?
When he departed for the trojan war—

Alack, my heart, that was a day in Argos:
The shore all dazzling with the grecian arms,
And every echo of the mountains, shouting
The acclamations of the warriors' cheer:—
He left you budding, large with royalty;
Where is the fruit?

CLYTEMNESTRA Arsinoe; you know,
That on the very night my child was born,
A menial traitor stole it from my side.

ARSINOE Had you not prov'd yourself more treas'nous prone,
By shameless tokens to your pamper'd slave,
That loyal theft had never been committed.
How could you think that there were none at court
To grudge his rising,—not one heart to feel
More for the monarch than his horse's servant?
Who did not fear from your infatuation,
The sacrifice of our true lawful prince?

CLYTEMNESTRA Oh! I am ruin'd, ruin'd, past all hope.

ACT I, Scene III

ARSINOE.

Alack, alack, where is that joyful stir,
That should await the victor from the field?
Where is the preparation for the feast,
The high adornments for the royal banquet?
Where are the musicians to swell the anthem,
And sound a flourish as the hero comes?
Here, silent, sullen Apprehension reigns;
And, for the wine that should flow at the board,
Blood shall be shed, and wailing rise for songs.

ACT I, Scene IV

ARSINOE *and* EGYSTHUS.

ARSINOE Audacious varlet, hast thou not yet fled?[20]
What incantation can the eagle charm,
That the usurper of his royal nest,
Shall not be torn and scatter'd to the winds?
Hast thou not heard the rushing of his wings,
And yet not slunk away?

EGYSTHUS Forbear, forbear,
And tell me what to do.

ARSINOE Go slay thyself—
Die with one death, for hundreds now await thee.
On every joint of thee, shall torture gnash;
And o'er thy quiv'ring remnants, shall the flames
Hiss as they feed.

EGYSTHUS Arsinoe, in mercy—

ARSINOE Thou grub, that dar'dst to crawl on royalty;
Better, far better had it been for thee,
To have been smother'd in the stable slough,
When thou, beneath a canopy of state,
Profan'd'st the breast where Agamemnon lay.

EGYSTHUS Was I to blame? By bribe and leer allur'd;
It was not I that dar'd,—I was besought.

ARSINOE Try what that plea will now avail thee, slave!

EGYSTHUS Would you had warn'd me but of this before.

ARSINOE Think'st thou, I wish'd to gain the prophet's fate,

---

20 A varlet can mean both a male servant or a dishonest man.

And for my boding, lie without my head.
But, now I speak. Thy hoofs are off me now.
And I am up again, and in my tower.
But, where is all thy rampant insolence,
Those high curvets, that so amaz'd the crowd?
Back, from the portal back, and give me passage.

ACT I, Scene V

EGYSTHUS.

This proud old fury will undo us.—
To fly, is now too late, for all the gates
And all the walls, are with spectators throng'd;
Waiting the king and trophies from the war.—

ACT I, Scene VI

EGYSTHUS *and* CLYTEMNESTRA.

EGYSTHUS Ha! come you here. Keep more aloof from me.
We stand upon the very edge of life.
Arsinoe has gone beside herself,
And threatens to betray.

CLYTEMNESTRA Cannot we fly?

EGYSTHUS Impossible! The town is all a-foot;
The roads are full, and every eye is wide.

CLYTEMNESTRA Would that Arsinoe could be prevail'd.

EGYSTHUS You always were too bold and confident;
I ever warn'd you to be circumspect.

CLYTEMNESTRA Had you been but content with private gain,
We had not fallen to this jeopardy.

But you still would have gaudy exhibition,
And ape the courtiers.

EGYSTHUS The fault was your's.
Why shower upon me, wealth, if not for use?
If we escape to night; before the dawn,
I'll off to sea, and never come again.

CLYTEMNESTRA Can you, Egysthus, break from me so freely.

EGYSTHUS Your husband is at hand.

CLYTEMNESTRA But, you, my lov'd—

EGYSTHUS Gods! cease this fondling.

CLYTEMNESTRA Ah! you love me not.

EGYSTHUS Better for me, had been your hate than love.
See what avails your gifts and your caresses.
My strawy pallet, yielded sweeter rest
Than your high couch, o'er-camopied with gold.

ACT I, Scene VII

ARSINOE, EGYSTHUS, *and* CLYTEMNESTRA.

ARSINOE Oh! wretched queen, regardless of thy doom.
E'en while the slaying hand is stretch'd to catch,
Thus, like a silly hen, safe in the sun,
To nestle fondly on a loathsome dung-hill.
If thou wilt welcome home thy lord with blood,
Go, wanton openly to all the court?
Why, with a half-seen leer or dubious smile,
Beget suspicion, since you seek detection?
Since you so dote upon your fated minion;
Go kiss him openly on the high-way;
Hang on his neck before the shouting rabble,

That all may know the lush of your lewd love,
And save grave justice from the amorous proving.
Ay, get thee gone, and curse thy brawny vigour,
That Death, so little will account to-night.

ACT I, Scene VIII

CLYTEMNESTRA *and* ARSINOE.

CLYTEMNESTRA Oh! my Arsinoe, what shall be done?
If flight could save, it is not in our power,
Nor will one suffer; all the three must die.
You were the confident, the minister;
Nor I alone, no: nor Egysthus only,
Will pacify the dreadful Agamemnon.
You, even you, that cherish'd him a babe;
And, by that claim, may think, perchance, to'scape,
Must bleed, unpitied, to appease his vengeance.

ARSINOE I was constrain'd; against my heart, I serv'd.
Thick fell my tears, and painful were my sighs,
On that dire night, when to your chamber, first,
I brought the overbold, o'er-weening groom.

CLYTEMNESTRA And think you then, by sacrificing us,
To save yourself?

ARSINOE Had you been wary wise,
Frugal in gifts, and ruled in your desires;
We had not come to this extremity!
But, all the nobles of the land beheld,
Your mighty love, descending in the gold.

CLYTEMNESTRA Yet, no one spoke, to me, as if they knew.

ARSINOE No! wherefore should they? You had other gifts.
What was the guilt to them, if you bestow'd
The boons that their obsequiousness implor'd?

CLYTEMNESTRA Why should the danger then, be greater now?

ARSINOE Why should it?

CLYTEMNESTRA Ay.

ARSINOE Because, with you, no more
Rest the rich motives of the courtiers faith.

CLYTEMNESTRA Yet, who, Arsinoe, but you alone,
Can tell, that more between me and Egysthus
Has ever pass'd, than may unslander'd pass,
Between a mistress and a worthy servant.
You shake your head. Well, grant I have been lavish:
It shows that avarice is not my foible.

ARSINOE Such boundless favour as you show'd to him,
And rapid transmutation from a slave,
To wealth that over-tower'd our proudest antients,
Are flagrant evidence that it was passion.

CLYTEMNESTRA What shall be done? ere many minutes fly,
The triumph will arrive.—What shall we do?

ARSINOE Save, if you can, yourself; as I will try.

ACT I, Scene IX

CLYTEMNESTRA.

Cunning, perfidious hag! thy insolence
Full truly proves, that I have stood on ice;
A slippery stead, deceitful and unsound!
But, why not her, as well as either, suffer?
She scruples not, to save herself by us!
Should we then pause to save ourselves by her?
But, how? There is not time; and were she hush'd,
Some other parasyte of patronage,

Will serve again th'ingredients for our death.
Ha! is there here a demon, prompting me?
If we could kill the king.—Tremendous thought.
My soul is curdled with the bare conceit!
But, if he live, I shall be slain myself:
And, how may this aspiring deed be done?
Or, by Arsinoe? Or, by Egysthus?
By posset, or by poiniard? Her, no more,[21]
Dare I confide in: and, if he should turn,
And give me up, to buy his own escape—

ACT I, Scene X

CLYTEMNESTRA *and* EGYSTHUS.

CLYTEMNESTRA How far is, yet, the army from the town?

EGYSTHUS By the last messengers, the van had come
On this side Mycenea.

CLYTEMNESTRA Well, Egysthus;
What think you now?

EGYSTHUS I only think of death.

CLYTEMNESTRA Whose death?

EGYSTHUS Whose death?

CLYTEMNESTRA Ay, whose?

EGYSTHUS My own and yours.
The witch. Arsinoe, will destroy us all.
Oh! had she died a month ago.

---

21 A posset was a British hot drink of milk curdled with wine or ale. Lady Macbeth (Shakespeare's *MacBeth*; Act II, Scene ii) used poison possets to drug the guards outside Duncan's quarters. A Poignard is a lightweight thrusting knife.

CLYTEMNESTRA You think—

EGYSTHUS What?

CLYTEMNESTRA If she had died a month ago?—

EGYSTHUS Well?

CLYTEMNESTRA You think then, that to-day is now too late?

EGYSTHUS What do you mean by these mysterious looks?
There's no one near us. Well?

CLYTEMNESTRA Alas! Egysthus;
We stand in imminent and deadly hazard.

EGYSTHUS I rue that e'er I fell within your sight.

CLYTEMNESTRA The past is gone: not Jove himself, can roll
The stream of time again towards the source.
Let us look around; perchance, in this dread whirl,
Some eddy may arise to bear us out.

EGYSTHUS Said you not, if Arsinoe were dead?—

CLYTEMNESTRA You are well built, and should be bold, Egysthus,
Had you but that courageous enterprize,
So needful to the lover of a queen,
We should not quake in such alarm'd amaze.

ACT I, Scene XI

EGYSTHUS.

What would the gagging of the saucy dame
Avail us now? Would not the death of her,

Save Clytemnestra; who, by it, might charge
Me with the murder, and so save herself.
Many there are among the palace swarm,
Who think, Arsinoe has been my dame.
I know the queen is crafty; though so fond,
That e'en to punishment, she clings upon me.
Yet may her sinister and subtile nature,
Egg her to this.—For me, there's no escape.
None, none! Had the king perish'd in the wars;
Or, by some sudden stroke, were yet arrested.—
The daring notion bursts like flame upon me.
And lights my fancy with magnificence.
But hark! the victor. Let his cymbals clash.
They ring in prelude to my swelling theme.

ACT I, Scene XII

AGAMEMNON, CLYTEMNESTRA, EGYSTHUS, *and* ARSINOE.

AGAMEMNON The captives now may, to the inner halls,
Bear their refulgent burdens, and the troops
Have quick dismissal. Let all hearts, to-day,
Exult in Argos; and, to those that mourn
For sons and husbands with the fallen brave,
Th' immortal tenants of the trojan plain,
Give double largess. Clytemnestra, here!

CLYTEMNESTRA Hail to my lord! all hail be to my hero.
O happy day; my second wedding day,
That gives, once more, to these long widow'd arms,
My Agamemnon, glorious and renown'd.

AGAMEMNON My Clytemnestra, still in all her charms!
I thought, ten years of anxious care, had blighted
The rosy of thy bloom; but thou art still,
Yea, rather, sweet, in fuller blow of beauty,
Than when we parted.

ARSINOE O my royal liege!

AGAMEMNON Arsinoe too! How hast thou fared, good nurse?

EGYSTHUS (*I hang upon the point of agony.*)

ARSINOE See this, Egysthus.

EGYSTHUS Heav'ns!

CLYTEMNESTRA Ay, true, my lord.
But sure, Arsinoe, we had time enough.
This gallant youth has claims upon your favour:
We'll take another time to speak of it.
Kneel down, Egysthus, to your royal master.
Now, my dear lord, we'll to the hall together;
Where you shall tell me all the tale of Troy.
Come, come Arsinoe, take Egysthus's arm,
And follow us. I'll serve you all I can.

ACT II, Scene I

ARSINOE.

Is it not sorc'ry that deceives my sight?
Or has my brain been drench'd with th' insane wine,
And I but fancy what I see and know?
Am I awake? Is this the vestibule?
Are these true echoes that resound my stamp?
Gods! I will charge her on the very throne,
Where she sits dallying at the king's right hand,—
To make me in the focus of the court,
Before the king and all the smiling nobles,
E'en to the saucy leering guards a show.
Some were that thought Egysthus dealt with me,
Now she has prov'd it, who shall dare gainsay?

But I will cry her wantonness to all;
I will amaze the hearing with her passion.

ACT II, Scene II

ARSINOE *and* EGYSTHUS.

ARSINOE How now detested! But thou art secure—
It was with me, with me, Arsinoe,
That thy nocturnal ravishments were spent,
I brought thee, slave, from curry-combing mares
To blandish majesty! I gave thee scents
To quell the odious odours of thy trade;
I shower'd the royal treasures on thy back;
I gave thee gems; e'en I, Arsinoe!

EGYSTHUS All true, good nurse; but cease this furious clamour.

ARSINOE All true! and dar'st thou smile and call it true?
Has Agamemnon come, and dar'st thou smile?
Thou that not many minutes since I saw
As lurch'd and cringing as a fact-found thief,
And wilt thou brag thyself my paramour?

EGYSTHUS If need will have it so. Look at this ring;
It is a jewel known to all the court;
You had it from the queen, and wore it often,
A glittering eye attracting star to all:
See where it shines enspher'd upon my finger.

ARSINOE I know, I know it well. Thy artful litter
Gave it to me; urg'd me to put it on.
And when I had some dozen times or so
Worn it abroad, she took it back again,
And now I see it on thy finger raying
As deadly as the eye of basilisk.
I cannot deal with such a sorceress.

EGYSTHUS Shall we be friends? Or will you still
Rave in defiance of such proof as this?

ARSINOE If I would screen, some other will betray,
And I shall suffer without serving you.
Wilt thou depart from Argos?

EGYSTHUS Without you!

ARSINOE What would my going hence avail to thee?

EGYSTHUS When I am gone you will accuse the queen.

ARSINOE And wilt thou stay? How! hop'st thou yet to share
Her lavish warmth, and Agamemnon here?

EGYSTHUS Were you but wise, all things might yet go well,
And turn of rich account, to you and me.
Come, let the courtiers take their laugh at us.

ARSINOE Avaunt from me. I thought thee in my power,
But thy familiar has unbound the cords,
And wrapp'd them round myself. What shall I do!

ACT II, Scene III

EGYSTHUS.

Now would this harpy, for her own success,
Crush me as if I were indeed a worm.
So climb they all at court, and why not I.
Ambition builds from ruins; and the fate
That gave me luring for a royal eye,
Inspires the gorgeous hope that draws me on
To lofty purposes. If the fond queen
Change not her fare and seek variety.—

ACT II, Scene IV

CLYTEMNESTRA *and* EGYSTHUS.

CLYTEMNESTRA Still rapt Egysthus, are you still afraid,
Want you the courage man to help me out?
Take heart and play the lover freely now;
I'll ask the king himself to give her dower,
And she shall marry you. Come be of heart,
Wed, wed her, man, and be a widower.

EGYSTHUS Is there no other way? Though she were dumb
As spade and turf can make her, some one else
Will spy and blab.—This night I'll leave the town.

CLYTEMNESTRA Ungrateful man that can so easy part!—
See'st thou not fortune stretching forth her hand
To pull thee to the golden eminence,
And yet wilt not take hold. O there are men,
Who, for the moiety of half thy chance,
Would dare the threats of fiery chimeras,
And through the volley of a thousand flames
Rush but to gain the height on which you stand.

EGYSTHUS But what is all while Agamemnon lives?—

CLYTEMNESTRA Is he immortal, inaccessible?
Invulnerable to the pointed steel?
Feels he no hunger, does he never thirst?—
Had I the motive friend that you might have,
And spice his supper!

EGYSTHUS But Arsinoe—

CLYTEMNESTRA Be it your study still to mar her entrance.—
Great gods! the king approaches! play to me
The begging sycophant, and haste away.

ACT II, Scene V

CLYTEMNESTRA *and* AGAMEMNON.

CLYTEMNESTRA O silly lout to ask so strange a thing;
There is full more than forty year of odds.
He must expect her surely soon to die.

AGAMEMNON Is that the youth for whom you claim'd my favour?

CLYTEMNESTRA The very same. Guess you what he has pray'd for;
But I forget—you know not who he is.
In sooth to say, 'tis a side-shaking tale.
The nurse, though old, is still, my lord, a woman;
And young Egysthus is a portly youth.
He has intreated me for your consent,
That he may wed Arsinoe.

AGAMEMNON What! he!

CLYTEMNESTRA Riches weigh well my lord against old age.

AGAMEMNON She must be craz'd and fallen far in dotage.

CLYTEMNESTRA You speak great truth. She is beside herself;
More than a month she has been chiding me,
To give my sanction; vainly have I spoken,
Yea pray'd her, oft, to quit her lewd intent,
At least, till your return. I should have else
Blush'd to have had the wedding in my house.
She is the laughing-stock of all the town.
When the glad tidings came that Troy had fall'n,
Gifts were distributed; and she received
The fairest ring you sent of all the spoil.
Some few short times she sparkled it about;

To-day I see it on Egysthus's finger—
That is not all. The old enchanted dame
Must have a rival, and be jealous too.

AGAMEMNON Alas! poor nurse! Who may her rival be?

CLYTEMNESTRA Can you not guess? Come try?

AGAMEMNON Indeed I cannot.
Ten years of busy and eventful strife,
Have worn away the frill of courtiership.

CLYTEMNESTRA Nay try to guess, and grow gallant again;
You must this martial sternness cast aside.
I will prohibit you the use of steel.
Gods! what have courtiers to do with swords?—
Nay, you shall wear soft velvet for your vest;
To-night you shall. What have you now to fear?
The am'rous glances of our ladies' eyes
Strike not so furiously as Hector's javelin.

AGAMEMNON But pray whose charms does fair Arsinoe fear?

CLYTEMNESTRA Ah true! will you not guess?

AGAMEMNON In truth I cannot.

CLYTEMNESTRA Who should it be, but she that still resists
Her wanton craze.

AGAMEMNON What! you?

CLYTEMNESTRA Your selfsame queen!
Nay do not laugh, for she has evidence.
'Why should the queen, if she were not in love,'
Says sage Arsinoe, 'oppose my bliss?' -
I could a hundred of her fancies tell you.

She is the merry-thought of all the court.
And when we have an empty hour to fill,
I'll call her confidents to make you mirth.

AGAMEMNON But who is he? How is her lover called?

CLYTEMNESTRA Egysthus.

AGAMEMNON True; pray what is he?

CLYTEMNESTRA Nay that
Is such a question I should ask myself.
She brought him, to me, as her relative,
And pray'd that I would notice him with favour.
But there are slanderers about the palace,
And I have heard, yet cannot credit it,
That he is of some very vulgar stock;
Nay, that his father was a menial slave.
Some viler envious still more assert,
And say that he himself was once a groom:
But this is wicked, and not credible.

AGAMEMNON I think so too. He has a gallant air.

CLYTEMNESTRA And is well spoken, and of pithy sentence.
To say the truth, the young man has his merits.

AGAMEMNON I'll speak with him, and should I find him worthy,
He shall have due promotion for his looks.
But see Arsinoe comes. I'll joke with her.

CLYTEMNESTRA Not for the world my lord. Now go you in,
Leave her to me, I must appease her fears
Nor is it modest for a man to speak
Of such a love as hers. Do leave me heart!

ACT II, Scene VI

ARSINOE *and* CLYTEMNESTRA.

ARSINOE And shall I never gain access to him?
How like a smiling harlot she appears!
O that a man so gen'rous and so great,
Should be cajol'd by such a false as this.

CLYTEMNESTRA How now, Arsinoe! why so sullen still?
All runs right smoothly, pray thee smooth thy brow;
The king is cheery, and laughs at your loving.

ARSINOE My loving, mine! How can you still persist?
The flattering lie will not avail you long.

CLYTEMNESTRA For your repute, things cannot now be worse.
By harming me, you cannot help yourself.
Though I were sacrificed, the world would say
You had your share; and you were confident!
Think well, Arsinoe, think well I say.
When you have once the fatal secret told,
No cunning then can charm it into rest.
You might as well by weeds and simples try
To place the yesterday behind to-morrow,
As to recall the shaft that you would shoot.
When it shall have departed from the bow,
The victims then must suffer.—Think I say.
How has the king been harm'd by what is done?
What print can he of poor Egysthus trace?
I seem as sweet and luscious to his eye,
As the untasted apple in the hand,
Would you persuade the pleas'd and cheerful child,
To cast it down, by crying grubs and worms?
Can he be hurt that knows not of his wound?
Arsinoe you are wise. Think well I say.

ARSINOE But will Egysthus quickly quit the court?

CLYTEMNESTRA Will you consent to sanction what is done?

ARSINOE How! tell the king he was my paramour?

CLYTEMNESTRA No: but ask leave to marry—nothing more.

ARSINOE And if the king consent—

CLYTEMNESTRA What if he do?

ARSINOE Better to send Egysthus from the land;
Think you not so?

CLYTEMNESTRA Yes, true; nurse you are right.
Will you request the king for leave to wed:
Then might I urge th' unfitness of the match,
And with entreaty pray you to refrain,
Bribing Egysthus to depart from Argos.

ARSINOE I yield, I cannot but submit to you.

CLYTEMNESTRA Dearest Arsinoe! counsellor, friend,
By this decision I'm thy slave for ever.
Ask what thou wilt. Have I no gem, not gift
That I may give thee, for this blessed mind;
See where Egysthus comes! alack, poor swain!

ACT II, Scene VII

CLYTEMNESTRA, EGYSTHUS *and* ARSINOE.

CLYTEMNESTRA More reverence, youth, remember I am queen;
Here beam your smiles, here on this op'ning rose,
Bestow O sun! the ray of amorous light.
Arsinoe has consented, will implore
The king's permission to espouse her swain.

EGYSTHUS Thanks sweet Arsinoe, now am I blest.

ARSINOE Pray mock me not. To-morrow be you ready—

EGYSTHUS So soon!

ARSINOE Rude insolent; to-morrow fly.
Be you not seen in Argos by the sun:
I may repent, and turn on you again.

CLYTEMNESTRA Come, come, no more; though lovers may fall out,
This is not time for bickering, dear nurse.
Egysthus, woo her with your sweetest breath,
While I inform the king of her desire.

ACT II, Scene VIII

ARSINOE *and* EGYSTHUS.

ARSINOE Presume not thou, though need has made it so—
And I must wear a masque before the king,
That I will light thee to her couch again.
Thy nights of majesty are all departed;
So hie thee hence to graze as thou wert wont,
And with some blouzy mate of thy degree,
Forget the dalliance of a royal bed.

EGYSTHUS Gentle, Arsinoe; ill words feed strife.
Our fates are mingled, and we should be friends.
If I am made of coarser stuff than kings,
And to be such is fault; is the fault mine?
If I was mother'd, like a whelp, in straw,
Say good Arsinoe if the sin was mine?
For well I wot, that to be lowly born,
Makes half a traitor of a man at court.
Pray what am I, that I should be so scorn'd;

Mulct of the grace that nature gave my form,
And spurn'd at as a draggled kennel cur.
What are you all that wear these lofty looks,
But blow flies, feeding on the state's sore back?
Have I not learnt the secrets of your game,
And known that with your stately stepping pride,
Ye are gynecocratic puppets all?
Taunt me no more, my haughty headed dame.
What, if I turn on you, and on the queen!
I stand in peril, but I know the worst;
And will no longer wheedle nor petition.

ARSINOE Did I not see, or was it but a dream,
You, you, Egysthus, cringing for my mercy?

EGYSTHUS But then, I thought not that your courtly craft
Would crush the friendless, to escape yourself.
My eyes are opened now to all your guile,
And I can look at death, with eye as firm
As he of Troy. But life is sweet to all;
As sweet to him that on bestrides the steed;
And my sweet life I will not cheaply lose.

ARSINOE Art thou, Egysthus, that light-hearted lad,
Who blush'd and linger'd, and was loath to come
To share the love and splendour of a queen?

EGYSTHUS Thy masque, Arsinoe; the king is here!

ACT II, Scene IX

AGAMEMNON, CLYTEMNESTRA, ARSINOE, *and* EGYSTHUS.

ARSINOE I had, my lord, a hearing to entreat:
Much cause have I to fear your dreadful rage.
I am, my lord, a very wretched wretch.
Fain would I speak, but terror mars my words;
I am not what I seem, nor what I was.

AGAMEMNON Thine is, dear nurse, a doleful case indeed.

ARSINOE This cruel woman! or what fitter name—

AGAMEMNON Kind, loving nurse, most cruel she has been.

ARSINOE Oh! my dear lord, if I had strength of grasp,
I would, this instant, give her doom myself.

CLYTEMNESTRA I told you true, she is beside herself.
Speak you, Egysthus, spare your true love's blushes.
Come, come with me, Arsinoe, and be calm.
I'll lead her hence, my lord, and calm her fears.
Come, come, I say; you shall have our consent
While I am with you and Egysthus here:
Be not afraid.—Restrain your jealousy;
Come, come, Arsinoe; come, trait'ress, come.

ACT II, Scene X

AGAMEMNON *and* EGYSTHUS.

AGAMEMNON Poor dame! Egysthus! one so young as you
Must sicken at this silly woman's dote;
Far better, man, to raise some other game:
Quit this mean scent and try the soldier's chace.

EGYSTHUS But I am poor and she has been my friend,—
Rais'd me, as I may say, quite from the earth,
And given me companionship with nobles.

AGAMEMNON Now this is good. I like this gratitude.
Perhaps, you hope she may die, quickly, off.
That honest smiling, pleases me, young man.
Think no more of this wrinkled carlin's passion;
I'll be thy friend, and give thy fortune help.

EGYSTHUS My royal lord, would I were worthy this.

AGAMEMNON Rise from thy kneeling. Wherefore are these tears?
Count me thy friend, and early claim my favour.

ACT II, Scene XI

EGYSTHUS.

Unhappy wretch; slave of remorseless fortune.
Thus on the threshold of my fell intent,
To meet this hospitable hearted friendship,
In him, in him, that I have so abused;
In him, alas! that I have doom'd to die.

ACT III, Scene I

CLYTEMNESTRA *and* EGYSTHUS.

CLYTEMNESTRA Good—good, all true; but then our danger think.
There is no choice, or he, or we must die.

EGYSTHUS I have already done enough of wrong.
Let this day pass; but by the morrow's dawn
I'll quit the shore, and bid farewell to Argos.
He has, unsought, shown me much gracious favour,
And but for the sour surfeit of the past,
I might have feasted with a cheerful heart.
Now am I like a sick man placed before
Rare treats and dainties that allure to taste,
For having foully fared; 'tis loathsome all.

CLYTEMNESTRA Egysthus, this is delicacy feign'd.
What is the favour that has wrought this change?
Has it not flow'd from my ill-answer'd love?
If you are thriving in the royal beam,
Who brought you from the chill ungenial shade?
Kings, like the sun, move in a distant sphere,
And those that prosper in their influence,
Must have the agency of meaner beings.

When the sun stoops from his meridian throne,
And turns the bending lilly to his eye,
Then will bright orbed royalty confer
Spontaneous fost'ring on a humble hind.
If you have this new debt of heart to pay,
I am the creditor; the claim is mine.

EGYSTHUS But are we not endanger'd deep enough?
This enterprize will but enthrall us more.

CLYTEMNESTRA If you have nerve of heart and strength of hand,
Virtue to think, and courage to perform,
We should, to-night, be only less than Gods,
Safe on the high olympian top of power.
But you so flinch and look for sculking 'scapes.—
Gods! I begin to rue that e'er I took
So mean a losel for my love and champion.

EGYSTHUS But when the stroke is struck, the courtiers then
May rush on me, and vindicate the blow.

CLYTEMNESTRA Fear not the sycophants, but do it well.
When it is done, they'll kneel and crouch to thee,
Like spaniel puppies that have done amiss.
I'll give command, that at the feast, to-night,
None come in armour, nor with warlike weapon,
As we have made the banquet for the peace.—
Bring you a dagger ready in your bossom.

EGYSTHUS It would be safer far to drug his drink.

CLYTEMNESTRA That cannot be without a confident;
And we have seen by curs'd Arsinoe,
What 'tis to traffic with such ministers.

EGYSTHUS I would that I had other means to live.
This task of blood is dreadful in the notion.

But strong constraint environs me around,
And I am clipt to the extremity.
Things come upon me with such rush and haste,
That wanting time, I want the power to think.—
Let me take breath; hurry me not so fast.
This speed of fate appals me. I'm as one
That steer'd his pinnace gaily in a river,
Feeling the force of some great cataract
Drawing him down: alarm'd, he sees the stream
That rippling murmur'd, changed to flowing glass,
O'er whose smooth silence slides the roughest wind:
Louder and louder nears the roaring fall.—
I will into my chamber for a space.

ACT III, Scene II

CLYTEMNESTRA.

This new felt penitence I cannot credit.—
Men that do injuries, regard their ill,
Like harsh injustice done against themselves
And seek to vindicate, by doing more.
He feigns reluctance, but his thoughts are firm;
His questions still have been to prove the way,
And once or twice, he slurr'd my constancy.
To doubt of me, whose fondness has o'erleap'd,
So far, the bound of all impediment.—
He never met me with that earnest warmth
Which my desiring bosom still required.—
His love of pomp and lordly equipage,
The fatal source of all our present fears,
Shows an ambitious demon in his breast.
What; if when I have placed him on the throne,
He change like other minions to their fond,
And strike aside the hand that raised him up;
Then am I lost again. Oh! fated fool.

ACT III, Scene III

ARSINOE *and* CLYTEMNESTRA.

ARSINOE Ha! in tears! What means this ominous shower?
Has then some other got the start of me?
How! does the king suspect?

CLYTEMNESTRA Arsinoe here!

ARSINOE Wipe as you will, I saw them falling fast.

CLYTEMNESTRA You have, Arsinoe, made me very wretched.
Better, far better had you brought a dragon,
Or deadly python, when you brought Egysthus.

ARSINOE Now, now, my words of wisdom come to pass.
But what has chanc'd so in a little hour?

CLYTEMNESTRA I cannot live, if he abandon me.
I struggled long to root his image out;
But deeper, still and deeper, it is fix'd.

ARSINOE And will you not consent to send him hence?
Well, drink to drunkenness; fill up the cup;
Forth to the street, and rant it out to all.

CLYTEMNESTRA The adder's bite, and the envenom'd bowl,
But pain us once, and soon we lie at rest;
While faithless love and fell ingratitude,[22]
Strike, every day, a new and sharper sting.

---

[22] The Errata corrects this from "gratitude".

ACT III, Scene IV

ARSINOE.

This sorrow was not meant for vulgar eyes:
Sudden and unexpected it has come.
Whence has it arisen? What can be the cause?
Egysthus?—His ingratitude?—How that?
He ever has been pliant to her pleasure,
And when he goes, it is for her he goes.
Why should she then dread his ingratitude,
Or faithless love? I understand it not.
Can they have quarrel'd?—How! for what, or when?
But here he comes, and I will study him.

ACT III, Scene V

EGYSTHUS *and* ARSINOE.

EGYSTHUS Where is the queen? I thought she had been here.

ARSINOE She was, but has retir'd. She seem'd distrest.

EGYSTHUS Said she not when she would again return?

ARSINOE You then expected to have met her here?
Her mind, indeed, seem'd sore and ill at ease.
You have, Egysthus, ill requited her.
For me, whom Agamemnon has so oft,
While yet a tender infant, milk'd and nuzzled,
With greedy playfulness upon my breast,
'Twas fit that I should roughly treat her lapse.
But you, who have her love and bosom shared,
To slight her so, is base ingratitude.

EGYSTHUS Has she again had confidence in you?

ARSINOE Confidence! how! What greater confidence
Could she entrust, than her own life and yours?

EGYSTHUS But did she tell you when she would return?

ARSINOE O you have something then to say to her?

EGYSTHUS You are inquisitive, Arsinoe.

ARSINOE Not I, Egysthus; but you look perplext.

EGYSTHUS To-morrow, nurse, I have resolv'd to go.

ARSINOE That we had settled. Have you alter'd since?
What dream of safety can entice your stay?

EGYSTHUS The king has shown me kindness.—Have you heard?
He is a noble and a gracious master;
My heart is yearning to become his slave.
Would that I could, be any slave but this.—

ACT III, Scene VI

ARSINOE.

There's more in him than going hence to-morrow.
Why feels he such compunction for the king?
What's this new confidence of which he spoke?
She cannot live, if he abandon her:
Then is he dearer to her than her life;
And dearer much than Agamemnon's life.—
And still he says, he will depart to-morrow.
Has she proposed to him, then, to remain?
Has she devised the murder of the king?
Horrible thought! O guilt, where is thy limit?
Since they have shut me from their councils now,

I'll play the spy; I'll be the ruler still.
I'll teach her yet, that she is in my power.

ACT III, Scene VII

CLYTEMNESTRA *and* ARSINOE.

CLYTEMNESTRA Still here, Arsinoe; but why so thoughtful?

ARSINOE Me-thinks your cloud has been of short duration.

CLYTEMNESTRA 'Twas but the drizzle of a passing vapour;
And in my clear and summer mind again,
The halcyon fancy spreads her gilded wing.

ARSINOE If you, with such a peril over you,
With such a deep and dreadful pit below,
And with an asp secreted in your bosom,
Can share the sun-shine of contented thought,
Let virtue perish, and all speed to vice.

CLYTEMNESTRA Thou speakest moral, good Arsinoe;
In sooth a preacher, proselytical.—
Was not Egysthus here?

ARSINOE Seek you him still?
The man has some contrition but in you.—
He has decided, and departs to-morrow.

CLYTEMNESTRA He spoke with you of his departure then?

ARSINOE He did: but he seem'd moody and distrest.
He sighs with strange compassion for the king?
What's in his fear? (*This pinches to the quick.*)

CLYTEMNESTRA (*Can she suspect? Can he have laps'd in ought?
Then are we lost. I'll prove her to the point.*)

Shall I not see him yet before he goes?

ARSINOE He did expect you, and you come for him.
Have you not had a pact to meet again?

CLYTEMNESTRA We had, Arsinoe; but if he go—

ARSINOE Did you entreat him to remain with you?

CLYTEMNESTRA What could I else? If he depart, I die.

ARSINOE Remain at court, and leave the king alive?

CLYTEMNESTRA Alas! unhappy me. (*'Tis as I thought!*)
The king himself persuades him to remain,
And also bids him think no more of you.
Why should he go? sure now there is no need.
Go find Egysthus; send him here to me,
I'd something further speak with him of this.

ARSINOE (*Though I could pawn my hand, there is a plot,
This thrice-shrewd traitor, still so dextrous shifts
The very lipping of the thing I seek,
Into some reason, fair and natural,
That makes me doubtful, even while convinced.*)

ACT III, Scene VIII

CLYTEMNESTRA.

Her stifled triumph and malignant glance,
Are proofs of her suspicion and deceit.
We must be speedy, or we are undone.
She said Egysthus spoke still of his going.—
But here he comes.

ACT III, Scene IX

CLYTEMNESTRA *and* EGYSTHUS.

CLYTEMNESTRA You tarry long Egysthus.

EGYSTHUS Saw you Arsinoe?

CLYTEMNESTRA Have you resolv'd?

EGYSTHUS Have you confided in her?

CLYTEMNESTRA No: not I!
Did you not speak to her, for she suspects?

EGYSTHUS I thought that you, perchance, had something said.
She will betray us—we shall be undone.

CLYTEMNESTRA Have you resolv'd?

EGYSTHUS I have no choice of will;
We are constrain'd, and more if she suspects.

CLYTEMNESTRA Come, pluck up heart; throw off this gloomy look;
Wear a smooth brow and cheat the world's eye.

EGYSTHUS But how, or when, shall we decide the deed?

CLYTEMNESTRA Did I not tell you at the banquet?

EGYSTHUS No!

CLYTEMNESTRA Then do it there. The hour is hast'ning on.

EGYSTHUS But there; I may not then approach the king;
He will be high in state, and far apart.

CLYTEMNESTRA Be you at hand, as we approach the entrance,
And when you see me take him by the arm,
And lift my robe, then strike; I will so wrap
Th' entangling drap'ry, as I link his arm,
That he shall not have chance to draw his sword.

ACT III, Scene X

EGYSTHUS, CLYTEMNESTRA, *and* ARSINOE.

EGYSTHUS Will Agamemnon then retain his sword?

CLYTEMNESTRA He, as the king, cannot do else, I fear.

EGYSTHUS Gave you command that none should come with swords?

CLYTEMNESTRA I did.—Are you prepared?

EGYSTHUS I am.

ARSINOE (*A dagger!*)

CLYTEMNESTRA Now let us part—you know the sign.

EGYSTHUS—The robe.

CLYTEMNESTRA Be bold and resolute; we cannot fail.

ACT III, Scene XI

EGYSTHUS *and* ARSINOE.

EGYSTHUS This night I sleep in open regal state,
Or in the deeper crimson of my blood.
Chaos and hell! hast thou been here and heard—
Detested witch; but if I kill thee now,

I shall precipitate myself to worse.
Hither, curs'd lynx, and die when I have time.

ACT III, Scene XII

EGYSTHUS, AGAMEMNON *and* CLYTEMNESTRA.

EGYSTHUS She has escap'd, and to the garden fled;
Had I pursued I should have been too late.

CLYTEMNESTRA Look where Egysthus stands; alas, poor swain!
Where is Arsinoe? She is not here.

AGAMEMNON Why think you of her? She will come in time;
Now let us in, for see the guests are placed.
What now?—

CLYTEMNESTRA This flowing robe entangles me,
Give me your arm, and let me take it up.

ACT III, Scene XIII

ARSINOE, AGAMEMNON, CLYTEMNESTRA, *and* EGYSTHUS.

ARSINOE Treason! murder! treason, my royal lord!

AGAMEMNON How now! release me.

CLYTEMNESTRA Strike, Egysthus, strike!

EGYSTHUS He has enough.

ARSINOE Alas! alas, too late!

CLYTEMNESTRA Stand back, ye daring and presumptuous crew,
Release Egysthus, and revere your master.

AGAMEMNON Tell me, Arsinoe, tell me what is this—

ARSINOE Bloody adulteress—

CLYTEMNESTRA Guards bear her hence.
I am the queen, and as you tend my will,
So shall ye have promotion and my favour.

AGAMEMNON O hell-born tygress, thus to welcome me!
The savage fierce are faithful to their mates,
But thou, perfidious, mak'st thy prey of thine.
'Tis done, 'tis done with me, I cannot rise.

EGYSTHUS I would have spar'd you, but to save myself.

AGAMEMNON hence! traitor, slave, and know I am thy king.
O thou chaste widow, that so mourn'd thy lord!

CLYTEMNESTRA Ay, play the man, the lord of the creation,
And scorn the failing woman for her sin.
'Tis but the sovereign element of males,
That nature honour'd with the sense of joy,
And privilege to range. Our serving sex,
Made for the use of free imperial man,
Must shut themselves in frozen chastity,
Like simple bulbs that winter in the soil,
'Till the ingerming season come again.
O it was meet that I your plant, at home,
Should spread my leaves and lift a flow'ry head,
To heav'nly sun-shine and the nightly dew!
Wives are not made of love's material. No:
We are but vessels, casting-moulds for men,—
While you lay glowing with your captive dames,
Or sacking towns to furnish wanton beds,
Thought you that nature slumber'd in my veins?
But such, forsooth, was my voluptuous lapse,
That only death or shameful degradation,

Could expiate the sin.—Learn ere you die,
That menial woman claims her half of love,
And wives deserted can assert the claim.

———

END.

LADY MACBETH, A Tragedy

Characters.

MACBETH
BAUDRON
SEATON
LADY MACBETH.
LADY

The stage represents an anti-chamber, in the castle of Dunsinane.

ACT I, Scene I

MACBETH *and* SEATON.

MACBETH Methought last night, as I lay on my couch,
I saw a silent-footed phantom pass,
In the pale likeness of my faded wife.
It look'd upon me sadly, and withdrew.
Such sights, 'tis said, betoken change and death.
Attends the spaeing hermit on our leisure.

SEATON He does, an't please your highness.

MACBETH Send him in.
Seaton, how fares the queen?

SEATON Still worse and worse.
The drousy poppy-draught has shut perception,
But ven'mous dreams creep underneath the sleep,
And sting her spirit as it fetter'd lies.

MACBETH Seaton, alas!—But send the culdee here.

ACT I, Scene II

MACBETH.

I would a little learn to know aright,
The dark precursors and ill-boding forms,
That make so wild my fated path of life.

ACT I, Scene III

MACBETH *and* BAUDRON.

MACBETH Nearer Baudron.—People say that Nature
Hath gifted thee with perspicatious sight,
To ken beyond our general human range,
The viewless mechanism of the world;
That thou hast held familiar colloquy,
With beings to our sense impalpable;
And learnt from them the index of events,
Far in the future and unknown of time.
I would discourse at large on this awhile,
And feed my fancy with thy mystic wisdom.

BAUDRON Your majesty confers great honour on me,
But age, dread sir, is all my faculty;
And that strange skill which rumour so proclaims,
Is but the art of noting, meeting things,

Fruit of a long variegated life.
There is in nature, sir, no accidents.
The boundless providential enginry
Still moves harmonious; and the augur-signs
Are but remote accordant parts, discern'd
Without the wedded wheels and linking chains.
For all the motions, in the frame of time,
Proceed combin'd, and rise from one great spring.

MACBETH What are those influential energies,
In their own nature substanceless, that take
Corporeal semblance;—Fate's dread oracles,
Who by the heralding of things to be,
Create the purposes that give them birth?

BAUDRON These, sir, elude the grasp of our gross wits:
They are like that occult intelligence
Which stirs between the ocean and the moon,
Known to exist by its effects alone.

MACBETH My dearest love! but wherefore come you here?
Go to thy couch again. Sweet, how is this
That thou dost wrap thyself so in the sheet?—
Let me take from thee that sepulchral omen.

BAUDRON Whom did your majesty just now address?

MACBETH Saw you it not?

BAUDRON Saw what, my gracious lord?

MACBETH A gliding apparition of the queen.
This is the second time it hath appear'd:
Last night it came dress'd in her chamber robes,
And gazing mournful on me, pass'd away;
But now it show'd the grim gaunt look of death,
And vanish'd, mantled in a winding sheet.

BAUDRON God save her majesty—

MACBETH What moves thee, Baudron?
Such metaphysical phenomenae
Are sights to which my eyes have grown accustom'd;
And I would know what is't that they foretoken.

BAUDRON Alas! the visions that amaze your highness,
Are the conceits of melancholy lymphs,
Mingled by nature in the glowing brain.

MACBETH But what do they portend? Interpret this:
Say wherefore twice hath the wan effigy
Of my perturbed, care-afflicted queen,
Risen to view a pale untimely ghost.

BAUDRON It was her wraith. The unknown minister
Who gives presentiment of coming woe,
Alas! forewarns that she is doom'd to die.
If it come thrice, call holy men around,
And let your wordly legacies be made;
For then the warding angel of your life
Resigns the keep to all subduing death.
The same day's sun that sees the queen a corpse,
O mighty king! shall never set to thee.

ACT I, Scene IV

MACBETH.

He cows my spirit, like the midnight owl,
The fatal prophet of the battlements,
That in his airy cloister overhears
The cloud-carr'd angels, hailing, as they pass
On dismal purposes of destiny.—
Oh what avails all regal exhibition,
While fest'ring in my bosom lies, the guilt
Of Duncan's blood, and Banquo's feller doom.

The priestly benediction, and the oil,
Nor all the ritual of the stone of Scoone
Can charm my eyes to innocent repose.

ACT I, Scene V

LADY *and* MACBETH.

LADY Macbeth, Macbeth, rid me of misery.—
All things in nature have become adverse
And daunt me out of life. The glorious sun,
That sheds to all delight and lumination,
Is the remembrancer of that dread dawn
Which show'd us Duncan, murder'd by our hands,
All horrible with his upbraiding gashes;
The beauteous moon that makes black night so fair,
With her chaste splendour as she climbs the sky,
Still wears, at rising, that deep blush of shame,
With which she look'd on Banquo's bleeding corse.[23]
The steller gems, the wakeful eyes of heav'n,
Show as they shine that they kept Argus watch
When we were busy at our midnight crime;
If one but glance at me an eager look,
The time has been when admiration pleas'd,
I shrink appall'd, and trembling shun the gaze;
The soothing phials of the doctor's skill,
Beget suspicion, for they bring to mind
The drugged wassail that seduc'd the grooms
To leave their royal charge in fenceless sleep,
To the foul carve of our ambitious waste;
Yea, my own hands, though costly scents perfume,
Are hateful by the old man's tainting blood;
And thou thyself, my former love and pride,
Art made so terrible by my remorse,
That I am madly urg'd by wicked fiends,
To think thy death would calm the hell that's here.

---

23 Archaic variant of "corpse".

MACBETH What potent sorcery transmutes thy nature,
Changing its high imperial arrogance
Into this weak and timid phantasy?
Rouse thee, dear wife, with that intrepid mind
Which when I shrunk appall'd in my intents,
Was wont by its courageous inspiration,
To nerve my soul with valour like its own.

LADY Oh! it hath perish'd with the pageant hope
That marshal'd my ambition. O'er my thoughts
Tremendous fancies fall like chilling shadows
On lonely spots by untold crimes accurs'd,
And a dread vista opening in the tomb,
Has shewn me horrors that dismay Despair
To cling to life.—I would but dare to die.

MACBETH And come the apparitions to thee too?

LADY As I, enchanted by the poppy's drouze,[24]
Lay on my couch, me-thought time had relaps'd
Back to that night on which we Duncan slew;
And as I would have wash'd my bolter'd hands,
Deep anguish pierc'd me, and in thought I died.
Exposed a space upon the regal bier,
The same on which, we falsely sad, adorn'd[25]
That good man's corpse; me-thought I was convey'd
With dues of heraldry into the vault,
Where all the royalty of Scotland rest,
And plac'd, dread punishment! by Duncan's side.
The requiem finish'd and the herald done,
The mouldy yawn of the sepulchre's gloom
Was clos'd, and I, left to resolve to dust.

MACBETH Terrible state.

---

24 Opium.
25 The Errata corrects this from "…falsely, sad".

Lady MacBeth

LADY Then did I hear around,
The churm and chirruping of busy reptiles,
At hideous banquet on the royal dead.
Full soon, me-thought, the loathsome epicures,
Came thick on me, and underneath my shrowd,
I felt the many-foot and beetle creep;
And on my breast, the cold worm coil and crawl.
When all that was corporeal had resumed
Its elemental essence, I became
Lost in vacuity and silent gloom;
A strange oblivion of sense, space, and time.
Anon I heard a trumpet from afar,
Swell with a sweet melodious invitation;
And saw ascend, millions of radiant forms:
Joyous they rose, and with them Duncan pass'd
More glorious than the Indian gem. His breast[26]
Was ruby-stain'd, Macbeth!

MACBETH Our guilty mark!

LADY Again the trumpet sounded; but so shrill'
So wild, so dissonant, so dread a shriek,
That I in terror started from the tomb,
And saw around me, all the wretched throng
That wrought on earth, catastrophes of sin.
Thou too wast there, but so, in form, transnatur'd,
That, fear to see thee, broke the spell of sleep.
Why stand you dumb, entranced in moody thought?

MACBETH The mind hath other vision than the eyes;
They are but windows in its tenement.—
Baudron is right, and these prospective sights,
Are but the distant coming-round of things.

LADY What is't you mean? Believ'st thou in this dream?
Shall we in death, lie conscious of the rot?

---

26 The "Indian gem" probably refers to the blood-red ruby, a naturally occurring gemstone in the Mogok Valley in Upper Myanmar (Burma).

MACBETH Calm thyself, love—I have a culdee priest,[27]
A wond'rous man, whose years exceed the round
Of a full century; and in his frame,
The faded energy of life renewing,
Puts forth a-fresh, the redolence of youth.
He hath deep insight of this complex world,
And knows the springs and pivots of events;
Th' invisible pervaders that controul
The secret lymphs which bear into the brain,
Those drifting fancies, that industrious Reason
Converts to scheme and knowledge practical;—
All these are known to him. He is a man,
A sage, of rare peculiar faculty,
And will unfold us, the pith of dreams,
And that imperishable consciousness,
Which wakes in sleep, and may in death survive.

LADY Shall we confess to him we kill'd the king,
And mew contrition like two silly urchins,
Sick with the surfeit of the pantry's spoil?

MACBETH My dearest partner of unhappy greatness!—

LADY Alas! Macbeth—but let us be ourselves,
And strongly master this enthusiasm.
Look at that table—see where ranged appears
The esculapian pageantry of death,
And then survey my blanch'd and haggard form,
Which, more than sickness, canker'd thought corrodes.
With these before me, and with this at heart,
I will wear boldly what I've dearly won:
What is done, is; and though my restless couch
Be nightly hideous with phantastic gorgons,

---

[27] The Culdees were members of ascetic Christian monastic and eremitical communities of Ireland, Scotland, and England pre-12th century. At Galt's time, Hector Boece's *Latin History of Scotland* (1516) makes the Culdees of the 9th to the 12th century the direct successors of the Irish and Ionian monasticism of the 6th to the 8th century.

Whose silent transit freeze me into death,
I wake to royalty, and will exact
The dues and reverence of our high estate.

ACT I, Scene VI

SEATON, MACBETH, *and* LADY.

SEATON My gracious lord,—thick-coming messengers
Announce the Southrons o'er the Forth advanced,[28]
Led by Macduff, the fiery thans of Fyfe,
And headed by young Malcom.

MACBETH Let them come
Here, by the bulwarks of our castle safe
And destiny impregnable, we scorn
The shock and larum of approaching war,[29]
Till Birnam forest come to Dunsinane.

ACT I, Scene VII

MACBETH *and* LADY.

MACBETH The times grow murky, and our star, dear love,
Hath reached the zenith. Fate's malignant orbs
Show baleful aspect in our horoscope,
And fortune, e'er it wanes, dims with eclipse.
Oh! we have found that every phase of fortune,
From the first faint edge, to the round bright full,
Marks the progression and the rise of care.

LADY These pallid fancies, better would become
My dreamy couch, than the bold circumstance
With which thou art assailed. Take courage thane;

---

28 The Errata corrects this from "Firth"
29 Larum is an obsolete form of Alarum, a call to arms—from the Old Italian all'arme ("to arms, to the weapons").

Rouse thee to war. Have not the weirds told,[30]
That as in panoply divine incas'd,
Thou art invulnerable to the steel
Of all of woman born? Assert thy fate.

MACBETH But I have lost the relish of renown,
And that which made the plaudits of the world
Richer than Music's voice, is mine no more.
O curs'd ambition; in pursuit of thee,
Thou unsubstantial iris of the brain,
I have so far into the desert run,
That all around me seems one blasted heath,
And still the phantom lures to wilder wastes.

LADY Come, come, forbear; this idle wonderment—
The dismal crimson that so coarsely glares
In the mind's painting of our secret deeds,
Time, with the mellowing varnish of success,
May yet appease, and the admiring good
Confess the merits of our great designs.
I was not form'd of sterner mould than thou,
Nor yields my couch a calmer sleep than thine;
Yet will not I, in this great game of life,
Spurn at the board because these shiftings vex me.
No, no, Macbeth; we cannot now return;
But on we must go—on, nor look behind:
And when a smoother brighter height we gain,
There plant those purposes of public weal
Which shall protect us; and within their shade,
Repose in honour, and lamented die.

MACBETH Yes: I will go, for I am pledged to it;
And like the homeless outcast prostitute,
Still heap the cairn of happiness with sins.

---

30 Weird is archaic Scottish for a person's destiny.

ACT I, Scene VIII

MACBETH, LADY, *and* BAUDRON.

MACBETH How now is this, if thou canst see afar
The forecast shadows of events, that thus
The pamper'd Southrons, with the fierce Macduff,
Invade out borders, and not I inform'd?

BAUDRON My gracious lord; such things particular,
In the vague range of your old slave's dim knowledge,
Have no precursor but the vulgar cry,
Which long and loud hath rumour'd preparation.

LADY His boding then is like the raven's croak;
A dismal gibber that but daunts the heart,
Without instructing where the danger lies.—
Send him away—we are ourselves, old man,
Deep-read in this lugubrious lore of fancy.

BAUDRON Fain would I shun these honour'd conf'rences,
But still his majesty commands me back.
If 'tis your highness' will, let me retire;
And in my lonely hazel-curtain'd cell,
Forget the court in charity to man.
O! holy Nature, thee I do acquit
Of all the foul that stains thy minion here:
How fair and nobly hast thou done thy part!
How bright and glorious shines the gen'rous sun!
How rich and soft earth's carpeting of flowers!
How fresh and joyous to the corp'ral sense,
The all-embracing dalliance of the air,
Contrasted with the base device of courts,
The dire cabal and mid-night work of blood.

MACBETH Traitor! what would'st thou? Darest thou jibe at us?

LADY Tut, my good lord, you do mistake the man.
He spoke but in a fit of calenture,
Th' impassion'd poetry of fond desire.—
Baudron, at night, I would converse with thee,
And learn the names by which to know the stars,
That, glittering, course the ocean of the sky;
And whence that radient messenger hath come, Which, nightly, in our zenith vault, is seen
With unknown splendour, firing half the heavens.
Till then, adieu.—Oh! shame to be so stirr'd.

ACT II, Scene I

BAUDRON.

The night advances to that horal bourn,
Where touch the wheels of yesterday and morrow,
And all the castle in defenceless sleep,
Fetter'd lies prostrate. 'Tis the chosen time,
When Rapine girds himself for enterprize;
Treason harangues his sworn conspirators
In dismal vaults, by torches darkly shown;
And Murder grasping firm the gleaming knife,
Stalks, with perturbed pace and soundless tread,
To the devoted couch.—Macbeth's a-foot!—
'Tis hallow-eve, and annual on this night,
Our youthful villagers, with rites and charms,
And old traditionary oracles,
Explore their destin'd boons of love and fortune.
Some say, that licensed from an antient date,
Th' imprison'd mischiefs roam at large to-night;
And in the gay unguarded heart of youth,
By juggling omens, raise perplexing thoughts,
That ravel all their future thread of life.

ACT II, Scene II

LADY *and* BAUDRON.

LADY Set down the lamp and wait without the door,
To give me notice when the king returns.
Have you heard, Baudron, what this wizzard is,
Whom they have brought again to vex his highness?

BAUDRON A solemn knave, that tampers with men's fears.
It grieves me much, that thus his majesty
Should lose the bent of his great character
In a mysterious passion to unfold
The seeds and secrets of the time unknown.

LADY This mournful lapse in my dear lord's brave nature,
While 'round the encompassing and trait'rous foes,
Deepen their files, awakes in me such fears,
That I could die for ease. Though I have felt
The pangs of birth, a mother's sleepless cares,
And watch'd my infant's couch with throbbing heart;
Sweet was that watching, and those cares were gentle,
And slight the pains to these I suffer now.
Thou art, I think, a good man; old and wise,
And much hast noted in this mazy world.
Oh! can'st thou not instruct me to redeem
Thy royal master from his cheerless bias,
And to untwine the gnawing serpent here?

BAUDRON In camp, and council, and the earnest strife,
Lie the true med'cine for the king's disease:
But solitude and sights of human woe,
And shelterless probation of distress,
Only, can minister to your relief.

LADY I have a tower lav'd by the salt-sea waves,
In whose horizon, never sail is seen,

Save the lone ferry-boat in summer calms,
Or stranded vessel in a winter's morn,
With her dead crew all frozen to the masts.
For such a place, so desolate and dread,
I would forsake these gorgeous rooms, and barter
The pomp and servitude around my throne,
If I might taste the Lethé of repose.

BAUDRON Alas! great lady.

LADY Wherefore so do you pause,
And sighing, wear a look so full of woe?
Why kneel you thus so pale? Rise, Baudron! speak!

BAUDRON To gain that sweet oblivious bliss of sleep,
Th' incumber'd spirit must unrobe itself
Of all the garniture of royal pride,
And pray Heav'ns mercy, as an alms, to grant[31]
The nightly down that eases daily toil.
For the proud throne, in ashes you must sit;
Change the rich crimson for a sack-cloth wrap;
Cast from your brow its unblest ornament,
The golden round, and radient type of power;
Yea, on the cold and parent earth degraded,
Confess the dismal secrets of your breast.

LADY Begone, old man: intruding prater, hence!

ACT II, Scene III

LADY.

Oh! shall I never know a calm again;
But like the sea, urged by the charter'd storms,
Bursting embarkments, still o'er pass my will
In billowy violence of troubled thought.

---

31 The Errata corrects this from "alm".

The old man, skilful, by Experience taught,
Discerns my soul's conceal'd and cureless sore.
Bu the afflicting cancer of remorse,
Makes scarcely half my sum of misery.
Macbeth, enchanted by his fatal credence
In the prognostics of bewild'ring lore,
Foregoes the occupation of a king,
For uncouth riddles and phantastic orgies,
Nor, with his wonted prescience, provides
For the dire shock of England's feudal streams,
Which flood the lowlands, to the Granpian's base;
And, swelling with the torrents of our clans,
Impetuous roll to insulate us here.
What, if by such fore-dooming negligence,
Young Malcom seize us in this last retreat,
And cage us for an ignominious show,
Like savages that feed on human carn!

ACT II, Scene IV

LADY, *and* SEATON.

LADY Seaton, what now?

SEATON The watch upon the hill,
See, by the moon-light, thick-defiling spears
Flick'ring among the boughs of Birnam wood.

LADY Hie to the king, and with some hasty speech,
Say, I entreat his special presence here.

SEATON His majesty approaches.

LADY Then, retire.

ACT II, Scene V

MACBETH *and* LADY.

MACBETH Be jocund, heart, good things await us still.
'Tis hallow-eve, and I have cast my fortune,
Which a brave seer hath shrewdly scann'd, and found,
Bating the vexing present's brief ordeal,
Nought but presumptives of prosperity.

LADY Fye; be a man, and leave such idle search
To cred'lous girls and boys professionless.
Or, if you will in signs and omens deal,
Survey the visible portents around.

MACBETH He has explained them all. The fiery star
Whose nightly apparition, o'er our heads,
Hath shed, of late, such fear into our breast,[32]
He has convinced me, by astrology,
Is the celestial swift-moving index
Of our hot-headed and far-follow'd foe.

LADY The dreadest prodigy of all the time,
Is the delusion that invests thy mind;
And like a spell, denies thee power to thwart
The rising adversaries of thy throne.
E'en while our castle and its mountain base,
Shake by the multitud'nous tramp of war,
No stir of preparation yet is heard.
All those fierce thanes, that favour'd our bold cause,
Who, roused in time, would still have faithful stood;
By this remissness from allegiance slip,
And make their peace with Malcom as he comes.

MACBETH There's not a man of them that shall be spared.
I'll taint the air, of the perfidious towns,
With traitors limbs for these desertions.

---

[32] The Errata corrects this from "heart".

LADY When?

MACBETH Ere Birnam forest come to Dunsinane.
Beneath our walls, the English epicures
Shall leave these curs that want the canine faith,
To crouch before us; but to crouch in vain.

LADY Infatuated hold! nor with the vaunt
Of wild mythologies and false predictions,
Think to repel our stern antagonists.
Know you, the watch upon the southern hill
Decerns th' advance of bright-defiling spears,
Glimm'ring behind the dark of Birnam wood,
Like the portentous streamers in the sky?
Awake, my thane, and shake thy drouze away;
Summon the council, and with manly charge,
Inspirit all that with our fortunes rank,
And boldly as you won, maintain the crown.
But I grow faint, and must to bed return.
The fervid malady, kindled by care,
Parching, makes head, and withers me to death.
Damsels, without!—Good night, my dearest lord;
Rouse thee to action.—Here; support me hence.—
Come Hope, to him, though thou hast fled from me.

ACT, Scene VI

MACBETH.

Spirit of valour, more than masculine,
Whom nor disease, nor circumstance can daunt,
But still when heaviest prest springs into strength,
And with its native royalty dilates
Still mightier than before.—Had I but men
Temper'd to half her pitch of energy,
The heav'ns might glare with prodigies of fire,
And hell's grim demons on the clouds appear,

In hideous panoply for Malcom's cause,
Nor change the pride of my collected soul.—
Who waits?—Send to me here the culdee priest.—
If all things be in one great frame conjoined,
The old man should by nat'ral symptom know
The issue of this crisis in my fate.

ACT II, Scene VII

MACBETH *and* BAUDRON.

MACBETH Thy look is weary, Baudron, and thine eyes
Seem as if grief had meddled with thy rest.

BAUDRON My feeble rag of life can ill endure.
The perturbation that besets me here.
These lengthen'd vigils prey upon my strength,
And I have used the charter of old age
Too freely, with her majesty, I fear.

MACBETH She will forgive thee—I will speak to her;
And when this traitorous investment's o'er,
Which circumscribes us to the castle here,
Thou shalt have 'tendance and the softest down,
To breathe in peace thy latter days away.—
But tell me, Baudron, by what marks to know
The fall and ebbing fortune of a king?

BAUDRON Then I must speak what prudence would conceal,
And things relate of harsh ungrateful note
To the sooth'd ear of flatter'd majesty.

MACBETH Fear not—my hearing has accustom'd grown
To tidings of adversity; and I
Can listen, to the worst that may befall,
Calm as the swain that hears the fading leaves
Whisp'ring that Winter hastens to disperse.

BAUDRON Alas! your highness hath already learnt
The dismal knowledge of your own estate.
The deep low discontents, throughout the land,
Have long been murmuring prelude to the clang
Of foreign war, which now so loudly dins
The dirge and knell of your departed power.

MACBETH But I am safe the weird sisters said,
Till birnam wood shall come to Dunsinane;
And by their greeting upon Forres moor,
Have I not found that they predict the truth?
Nature hath turns that in the plainest course
Perplex our wisdom: and may I not hope,
Who hath received such proof of special fate,
That those sad signals which are wont to show
Disast'rous change to others, shall to me
Prove but precursors to a passing care?
As night is harbinger to the gay morn,
And boist'rous Winter heralds forth the Spring.

ACT, Scene VIII

MACBETH, SEATON, *and* BAUDRON.

MACBETH Well! what new chance hath so amaz'd thy wits,
That they seem ready in thy straining eyes
To leap from some great jeopardy?

SEATON My lord,
The tartan'd Celts that from the western isles,
And the fierce Donalds from Benevis' side,
Who lay upon the heath, have left their ground,
And with th' outrageous insolence of pipes,
Are seen by all the wardens on the walls,
Precipitously hurrying to the foe.

MACBETH Well, let them run; I little priz'd their faith.
These mountain aborigines have been

The stubbornest to tame, of all beneath
The antient scepter of the scottish kings.
This waste in loyalty smites the great arm
Of royal vengeance with paralysis,
And makes the tasks that press upon our time,
Of heavy labour and uncertain fruit.—
Seaton, why stand you here?—

SEATON I have but half
The errand of my coming-in reported.

MACBETH What hast thou more? Who else deserts from us?

SEATON By urgent summons from the queen herself,
The chieftains lodged within the keep attend
Your highness' presence in the council-hall.

MACBETH We shall be there anon—Seaton command
The armourer to have my mail prepared.

ACT, Scene IX

MACBETH *and* BAUDRON.

MACBETH My soul is kindling, Baudron, for the fight,
And they who dare disturb the lion's den,
Shall rue the boyhood that provokes his rage.
I was a famous soldier in my day,
And my heart leaps for this impending strife,
As when the trumpet call'd me up to arms,
On the proud dawn of battle. But I feel
That eighteen years of vexing monarchy,
Have cool'd the martial ardour in my heart,
And the entanglement of crafty care
Has long destroy'd the frankness of my youth.

BAUDRON Alas! dread sir, so is the course of life.
There have been men that nature meant for heroes,

Lady MacBeth

So everborn by fortune's accidents,
That at their exit from the world's great stage,
Instead of plaudits, and the full resound
Of admiration irresistible,
They have been followed by the damning hiss,
So ill and slovenly they did perform.

MACBETH Would I had still but a free soldier liv'd,
And been unstain'd by any other blood
Than the red trophy of my country's foes.

BAUDRON Why starts your majesty?

MACBETH See you not these?

BAUDRON Where? What?

MACBETH It is the selfsame heraldry
With which the gentleDuncan was convey'd
To the last mansion of the scottish kings!

BAUDRON I see it not—Alas my gracious lord!—

MACBETH What can this dismal pageantry betide?
Another and another! still they come
Solemnly marshall'd—ha! the sable bier!
It stops—and see the sheeted dead thereon
Doth raise itself. My wife!— 'tis all away.—
Baudron—

BAUDRON What would your highness?

MACBETH Good old man,
To live so long and fear no sights like these.

BAUDRON My royal lord—

MACBETH Baudron, didst thou not say,
That if the spectral vision of the queen
Rose thrice before me, her decided death
Should mine foretoken, on the selfsame day?
Now thrice the airy semblance has appear'd,
And this time with such charnel exhibition,
That none may question what the sign portends.

BAUDRON The lonely shepherds in the isles forlorn,
And pale enthusiasts bred in silent glens,
Have oft by metaphysical discernment,
Seen these sad shows, and verified the bode.

ACT II, Scene X

LADY, MACBETH *and* BAUDRON.

LADY Macbeth! Why start you so aghast, my thane?
Why touch you thus, and look to the old man?
Thy cheek is ashy, and thy restless eye
Denoted strange fear and doubt mysterious.

MACBETH Alas! the constancy of my sad mind
Is put to dreadful proof. Around me rise
Such prodigies and omens of dismay,
That were my spirit fram'd of temper'd steel,
And to the stroke invulnerably firm,
I need must quake to witness what I see.

LADY I left him hopeful—tell me how is this?
Hast thou been with thy priestly exhortation,
Cowing the hope that he so much requires?

MACBETH Oh! there are things in this mirac'lous world,
Which time, nor learning, never can explain.

LADY Good, good, my lord—but to the council come;
Malignant Fortune wins by our default.

This fatal sadness, the unmans you so,
Would better suit the weak of my disease.

ACT III, Scene I

LADY.

Where may I shun this omnipresent horror
That scares my every sense, and fills my soul.
My shadow turns the monitor of guilt,
And, pointing with its unsubstantial hand,
Seems the precursor of avenging justice;
While the shrill ring of arms, distributing
To all the servants, sounds as awfully
As the deep-tolling of a passing bell.

ACT III, Scene II

LADY *and* SEATON.

LADY What now, good Seaton; what new ill hath chanc'd?

SEATON The wood of Birnam has begun to move.

LADY What says the king?

SEATON He was disturb with ire,
That men should say a thing so wry to nature;
Anon his choler fell, and he appear'd
Like some prime merchant, who receives the news
Of all his fortune perish'd in the waves.

LADY Alas, alas,—go, bid my maids attend.
The fiery fever thrills through all my frame,
And darts delirium to my tingling head.

ACT III, Scene III

MACBETH *and* LADY.

MACBETH The wood of Birnam comes to Dunsinane!

LADY Art thou Macbeth, and wear'st these looks of fear,
E'en while the men of Malcom, from thine eye,
Hide their pale faces with the forest boughs?
For such must be this daunting miracle.

MACBETH But they that did forewarn me of the sign,
Bade me to dread no danger till it came.
Behold it doth arrive.

LADY They warn'd thee well:
But the prediction has been read amiss.
We should have stood expecting fortune's change,
And been so ripe in all the means of war,
That Birnam forest, moving from its site,
Should e'en have found our full matur'd array,
Prepared for chances supernatural.
But my enfeebled limbs foregoe their office,
And to my couch I must again return.
Go to thy men, and with thy wonted fire,
Inflame their bosoms to th' accustom'd zeal.

ACT III, Scene IV

MACBETH.

Why should I, thus, be still the toy of fortune,
While my own hand contains the means of riddance?
This is the key that may unlock the door,
And show me all the secret things of fate.
But wherefore is it, that I dread its use?
I, who so oft in pride of youthful blood,

Have all the tumults of the battle dared,
As 'twere, to force, outrageously, to enter
The undiscover'd labyrinth of death,
Though them I knew not this pursuing fear;
Nor had incited, thus to hunt me down,
The hungry vengeance of vindictive men.
Oh! while so chased, am I afraid to fly,
Since tarrying here, ensures a certain woe;
And using this, will bear me safe away.
To be imprison'd in this mortal cell,
And know the boundless liberty without!
To be so manacled, and yet to shrink
From the short tingle of the setting free!
Oh! to what cowardice the dross of flesh
Degrades the noble element of man.
Seaton, without; who waits, Seaton, I say?

ACT III, Scene V

MACBETH *and* SEATON.

MACBETH What mean these acclamations from our men?

SEATON The enemy have thrown the branches down,
And round the castle, show us all their war;
Light-kindled spears and crests of waving plumes,
Which your bold lieges on the walls and towers,
Welcome with gay defiance.

MACBETH Hearts of gold!
Give them my thanks. In their courageous note,
I heard the voice of other times resound.—
I'll wear to-day, the armour I had on,
When, for my carve at the Dane's carnage feast,
I gain'd new honour from the good king Duncan.
Ha! will my every thought still turn on him,
And each slight motion of long unfelt joy,
But stir the wounds of guilty agony!

ACT III, Scene VI

BAUDRON, LADY, *and* MACBETH.

BAUDRON O spare me, spare, dreadful majestic dame;
Tremendous lady, spare my feeble life.

MACBETH Hold, dearest, hold: what would'st thou with this dagger?

BAUDRON Thou shalt in sulphur burn for sorcery.
He holds cabals and traffickings accurst,
With the malignants that make murk the mind;
And doth suborn them to beset my couch,
With bosoms smear'd, and visages all grim;
Like dead men rising from their mid-night beds.

MACBETH Hast thou then, Baudron, pow'r with imps of ill?

BAUDRON My lord, my gracious lord; her highness' brain
Yields to the fervour of the fever's rage.

LADY I feel his devilish conjurations work,
Constraining me by terrible conceits,
To crawl dishevel'd, like the eastern king,
Whose locks were matted by the rain of heav'n.

MACBETH If thou hast cunning to concoct the thoughts
To these persuasions, old man, stay not here;
Hie thee to Malcom's camp, and there employ
Thy subtile metaphysics to dismay.

LADY Look there, Macbeth, where his black art hath brought
That pale, thin, meek, old, hoary king asleep,
So like my father when I saw him die.
Anon, anon, the spell doth work apace,
And the botch'd bosom shows all foul with blood.

Whose are these gory sacrilegious hands?
One holds a dagger, and the other gropes,
As 'twere, to find the corpse.—They are my own!

ACT III, Scene VII

BAUDRON *and* MACBETH.

BAUDRON It is, my liege, the fume of the disease,
Clouding like vapour her serene of mind:
The sun of reason fails amidst the gloom.

MACBETH She was not wont to see these spectacles;
And since thou hast been here, free friend with us,
We have, such air-embodied horrors seen
Rising before us, in the cheerful wake,
Like incantations of the wizard Sleep,
That day has grown as hideous as the night;
And baleful Memory, witching nurse of Fancy,
Mingling the caldron of perturbed care,
Gives aspectable form to dreadest things.
Again, I say, if thou hast wrought this change,
Depart our threshold. But if thou art man,
Stay; for the genius of thy antique lore,
Is touch'd with mystery, so finely wild,
That I could listen, had I leisure ease,
Far rather to thy hypothesis,
Than to the cadence of the minstrel's song.

ACT III, Scene VIII

SEATON, MACBETH, *and* BAUDRON.

SEATON My lord, the enemy move to the walls,
Th' impetuous thane of Fyfe before the van,
Waves his claymore, and urges to the gate.
I saw him turn impatient as he came,

And drag with fierceness, which brook'd no delay,
The batt'ring engines, lab'ring up the steep.

MACBETH Let them come on, and all of woman born.
My soul is kindling, and from every tower,
We will such hurl of furious vengeance hail,
In barbed shafts and missiles, wing'd with flame,
That they shall rue their trait'rous appetite,
To break the fold where majesty lies pent.

ACT III, Scene IX

BAUDRON.

Poor miscompounded, miscommissioned man,
Enrich'd with valour and the heart's best ore,
But so mixt up with fellest cruelty,
As still to have affinity for ill.
While I rejoice that, thus, the ruthless king,
Whose scepter, grimly clutch'd, has made the land
Quake to its utmost ocean-beaten cape,
Already feels the retribution close,
My bosom yearns afflicted for the man;
As when a father mourns the dismal end
Of his o'er-fondled, long-unchidden son.
Ill-starr'd Macbeth! had destiny withheld
Thy high enthusiasm from the sway
Of thy arch-human wife, who, sternly proud,
Amidst the storms of fortune and disease,
Stands like a rock, around whose clouded head,
Gleam fires from heav'n, while billows dash the base;
Perchance, O hapless, to thy trophied name,
The long processions of posterity
Might have, admiring, look'd and pass'd improv'd.
Hark! 'tis the engines thund'ring at the gates.

ACT III, Scene X

LADY *and* BAUDRON.

LADY I will not, damsels, have the doctor more.
Ha! coreless stump of age, how is't that thou
Appear'st unshaken, while the royal trees
Feel the rude lopping of the tempest's force?
Again, again; the house itself grows craz'd,
And by this dreadful batt'ring trembles all.
Ye jerking vaults have ye turn'd traitors too?
Down, down at once, incairn me while a queen,
That I may 'scape the ignominious pelt
Of rabble execration. 'Tis ours that shout!

ACT III, Scene XI

SEATON, LADY, *and* BAUDRON.

SEATON The foe retires, for havoc, eagle-fang'd,
Pounces resistless where the king appears,
And none withstand the rage. Wounds to our men,
Become, as 'twere, new energies to life.
Their valour burns with an intenser heat,
By the quick stirring of their fomen's steel.
The king shall yet be king.

LADY—Did'st thou think else?
What! had'st thou con'd in previous cogitation,
The phrase and suppliency meet to earn
The base prolongment of thy cringing life?

SEATON I have, dread madam, ever faithful prov'd;
Nor aught, that duteous service might desire,
Has been neglected in my willing tasks.

LADY Rise from thy knees.—Alas! my troubled brain,
With vague and fearful rumours all perplext,
Betrays me often to forget myself.

ACT III, Scene XII

LADY *and* BAUDRON.

LADY Can'st thou, old man, to changeful life inured,
Teach me the art to keep in even flow,
The method of my thoughts. I feel myself,
Like one forced far by currents from the shore,
In some small bark, that the great billows toss,
On the white curling of their mighty mains;—
No will of mine availing.

BAUDRON Happy they,
Who as they toil along the flat low sands,
To pick their pittance from the tide's refuse,
Can see, unwishing to partake the voyage,
The cheer'd departure of the gaudy ships,
Whose swelling sails advance to meet the sun.

LADY Thy pale morality would better suit
The meek dejection of a pining fair,
That mourns her high-born lover's faithlessness,
Than the stern grief of a devoted queen.
I pray thee, Baudron, vex my heart no more.
My fancies thicken as the tumults rise,
And whirl in frantic eddies to despair.

ACT III, Scene XIII

LADY, MACBETH, *and* BAUDRON.

LADY How now, Macbeth, what dost thou from thy post?
Forth to the men; nor in thy fury slack,
'Till thou hast swept with iron besoming,
The impeded course of our regality.

MACBETH My fate is verified. No man of them
Withstands the flash and tempest of my sword.

Back from the gates they all recoiling roll,
A bloody rubbish: wounded, dead and dying,
Lie heap'd a hideous pile.

LADY My valiant king!
Back to the revels of grim Mars again,
And gorge thy valour.

MACBETH Ah! my dearest love,
I have, alas, encountered there a foe,
More terrible than all of woman born;
And ere again I breast the battle's surge,[33]
I would hold parley with the old man here.

LADY Fye, fye, Macbeth, thou dalliest with our fate.

MACBETH I oft in childhood roamed the haunted glens,
And heard the rustle of the bard-sung ghosts;
In bolder youth, all lonely, I have scaled
The windy summits of our wildest hills,
And heard the whisp'ring of contriving sprites:
But, nor in childhood, nor in pensive youth,
Nor when the sisters on the blasted heath,
With supernatural prediction hail'd;
Nor all the spectral visions I have seen,
By night, or noon, or in the witches' cave,
Ere struck such chill into my daunted heart,
As the creations of my guilt to-day.

LADY By what new goblin hast thou been amaz'd?

MACBETH Each wound I gave, seem'd Duncan's gash renew'd;
Each groan I heard, sounded like his expire.
Whene'er I turn'd, to praise my valiant men,
In their brave exhibition, I discern'd
Th' accusing semblance of the murder'd Banquo,
As when he fought with me against the Dane.

---

[33] The 1812 edition has "battle s", the apostrophe has been restored here.

All the encrimson'd secrets of my life,
Glar'd in my sight; and though to madness driv'n,
I rush'd to meet destruction every where,
The bolts flew harmless o'er my charmed head,
And pointed spears fell blunted from my mail.
Oh! that which promis'd me a safe long life,
Inflicts more anguish than a thousand deaths.

LADY There is no remedy for us, Macbeth.

MACBETH Help, help; she dies!—fly, help—the doctor; fly.

LADY He has no lenitives for my disease;
Nostrum nor simple can remove my pain.

ACT III, Scene XIV

SEATON, MACBETH, *and* LADY.

SEATON My lord! my lord! Macduff has storm'd the gate!
The men cry for you; and the rushing foes
Fill all the court.

MACBETH Well, well, go save thyself.

LADY Art thou a king, Macbeth?—Stay not for me;
I do begin to freshen and revive.
Away my thane, and with the joyous news
Of thy success recruit me.—Thane, away.

ACT III, Scene XV

LADY *and* BAUDRON.

LADY What see'st thou, damsel, to look at me so?
Give me some drink, some strong restorative.
A clay-cold chill is creeping to my heart—

Where the parch'd devil of the fever sits,
And craves the cooling freshness. Give, O give.—
But all the welling fountains of the hills,
Cannot allay the deadly thirst that's here.

BAUDRON This wat'ry bev'rage slightly tinged with wine—

LADY Ha! wretch— 'tis blood!—

BAUDRON Alas! they all have fled,
In panic horror at the howl she gave,
And left her, dreadful doom! to die alone.—
Hither ye pale appall'd. This mighty dame,
Is now as harmless as the sludge, that's cast
From the brief trenchment of a baby's grave.

ACT III, Scene XVI

MACBETH, BAUDRON, SEATON, &c.

MACBETH Come, stand apart, and let me look on her.
Tears ill would suit the stern magnificence
That should attend thy bier: such drops as these
Red trickling from my sword, should fall for thee.
For thou wast made of such courageous stuff,
That the heroic when compar'd with thine,
Prov'd minor metal form'd for meaner use.
Yes, noble lady, thou hast died a queen;
Invidious Fortune would have bent thee down,
But thy undaunted spirit aw'd the fiend,
And with triumphant royalty has left
Its frail corporeal mantle as it rose,
To rouse me to great things. Baudron thou said'st,
That the same sun that saw the queen a corse,
Would ne'er on me bestow a setting beam.
Lo! there she lies!—And hark, the storm without
Thunders prelusive to the dread finale.

Fate do thy worst, I dare thee to the beard;
Nor life, nor crown, nor victory, nor fame,
Inspire my great intent. For death I fight;
And will the black tremendous trophy gain,
Ere this last consummating day be done.
Pull down the royal standard from the tower,
And in its stead unfurl the funeral pall;
The ensign of my cause. To all adieu.
Dull guestless mansion of my love farewell;
I go to meet her, though it be in Hell!

———

END

ANTONIA, A Tragedy

Characters.

FERDINANDO
CARRAVAGIO

ANTONIA
TERESA

The stage represents a magnificent saloon, adorned with paintings.

ACT I, Scene I

ANTONIA.

My heart is full of heaviness and fear!
I blush and tremble like a guilty wretch;
And yet of guilt and shame what have I done?
Last night my lord was late abroad with friends,
And save the servants with him, all the house
Was gone to rest ere I had sought my room.
As wont my chamber door was left unbarr'd;

But I was sunk to sleep before he came.
He spoke not to me, and before the dawn
Departed hastily while yet I drouz'd.
Did he not come? Have I but strangely dreamt?
O righteous Heav'n, drive from my madding brain
Th' opprobious fantasy that seeks admission.

ACT I, Scene II

ANTONIA *and* TERESA.

TERESA Come my dear lady, do not weep so sadly;
The count has promis'd to be here at noon.
It was, 'tis true, a wayward prank of him,
So on the sudden to set out for Florence.—
But these deep-drinking English—

ANTONIA Oh my heart—

TERESA Though he were lost you could not sorrow more.

ANTONIA Oh! he is lost to me—and I am lost—
Undone, undone; for ever, evermore!

TERESA Why yield to such a passion of despair?

ANTONIA Not to inform me!—

TERESA—All a riot flight.
'Twas Ferdinando begg'd to come and tell,
Else had we still been in a deeper trouble.

ANTONIA Ha! Ferdinando begg'd!—Horrible slave!
To traffic so between my lord and me!
Where slept the angels of the pure and chaste,
When the foul profanation was perform'd!

ACT I, Scene III

TERESA.

Alas, poor soul! she takes it sore to heart;
And yet, methinks, it was no deadly sin,
For count Urbano, in a frolic fit,
To see his foreign friends safe to the town.
Had he but sent a loving note to her—
But wine that with an uproar steals the sense,
Has no respect for duteous courtesies.—
Why should she rage at Ferdinando so?
He did right well, and seems to deeply mourn
The rash excess that so betray'd his master.

ACT I, Scene IV

FERDINANDO *and* TERESA.

FERDINANDO How does my lady?

TERESA Sadly, weeping sad.
'Tis very strange that she should so bewail.

FERDINANDO Does she suspect?

TERESA How! what should she suspect?

FERDINANDO Why I did not inform her when I came.

TERESA And did you not?

FERDINANDO No; for she was asleep.

TERESA How knew you that? Went you into her chamber?

FERDINANDO She made no answer when I rapp'd the door.

TERESA So then you open'd it, and dar'd to enter!

FERDINANDO What could I else?

TERESA You found her then asleep?

FERDINANDO Why look you at me so inquisitive?

TERESA That you should dare to be so bold as enter.
What said you to her to affright her so?

FERDINANDO Nothing.

TERESA Nothing! how? When you told her—

FERDINANDO —Ay.

TERESA Perhaps she did not hear?

FERDINANDO I think she did.

TERESA And you came out, not knowing if she knew?

FERDINANDO I did. What said she when you spoke to her;
When you inform'd her that our lord was gone?

TERESA Are you then sure she heard you not last night?

FERDINANDO I cannot tell. But what says she to-day?

TERESA Why ask you me so often? She is sad;
Sad as a new-made widow for her lord.

FERDINANDO I think I will to Florence to my master.

TERESA You will to Florence! wait upon our lady,
And tell her better than you did last night.

FERDINANDO What can I more? You have already told her.

TERESA I pray you go.

FERDINANDO And is she much distress'd?
Think you she will be angry when she sees me?

TERESA Why should she? Sure it was no fault of yours?

FERDINANDO The door was open, and I thought she heard.

TERESA Thou thought she heard!

FERDINANDO In truth I did, Teresa.

TERESA 'Tis very strange!—Go, get you hence, audacious.

ACT I, Scene V

TERESA.

There is some hideous mystery in this.—
She is almost distracted in her thoughts.
Yet is this wretch that was the messenger
Not certain if she heard him when he told.
For then he says she slept; and yet he thinks
That she did know of his presumptuous entrance.
Why should he fear her anger? Or why she
So kindle to distraction at his name?
Heav'ns, could the varlet be so bold!—
Could she in sleep, unconscious, be betray'd?
O wretched lady! O ill-fated fair!
So chaste, so excellent to thy lov'd lord.—
But let me not to such conceptions yield;
If she has been a partial hypocrite,
And heard the curs'd intruder in the room.—
The painter here! why has he left his work?
It is not usual with this studious man.

ACT I, Scene VI

TERESA *and* CARRAVAGIO.

TERESA What seek you signor Carravagio here?

CARRAVAGIO The countess wants you; she is very ill.

TERESA She parted from me but few minutes since,
And then complain'd not: only griev'd to think
The count so hastily had gone to Florence.

CARRAVAGIO Has nothing else befallen?

TERESA As I hope.
Think you that she has other cause to grieve?

CARRAVAGIO Something most fatal has occurr'd last night.
The countess seem'd as one would like to paint:
Lucretia when she had escap'd from Tarquin.

TERESA She mourns this luckless frolic of her lord.

CARRAVAGIO No, no; her grief is of a deeper wound.

TERESA Why signor Carravagio think you so?

CARRAVAGIO The painter's art instructs him to discern
The movements of the spirit in the face.
Before this anguish, keen and terrible,
She still has worn a countenance serene;
Modest, though buxom, and though blooming, mild,
Like cheerful Dian waiting for the day.—
But go, she needs you. Sooth her if you can.
Send Ferdinando, if you see him, to me.

ACT I, Scene VII

CARRAVAGIO.

The fellow has a dark lascivious leer,
So blended with a sober villainous air,
That he assists my fancy as I draw
The story of Susannah and the elders.

ACT II, Scene VIII

CARRAVAGIO *and* FERDINANDO.

CARRAVAGIO How now, friend Ferdinando. Know you not
That you have kept me idle all the morning?

FERDINANDO I was not hired to act a jewish priest.
Sir, I have other duty in my place.

CARRAVAGIO The count has said whene'er I wanted you,
All other service should be then postponed.

FERDINANDO But I have business, sir, in town to-day.

CARRAVAGIO Does not the count return?

FERDINANDO I cannot tell.

CARRAVAGIO Were you not with him at the Villa Fresca?
I heard you were, and came home late last night.

FERDINANDO Who told you that?

CARRAVAGIO The countess did herself.
Alas, poor lady! she is much distress'd.

FERDINANDO Is she?

CARRAVAGIO She is knave!—Hast thou done aught wrong?

FERDINANDO What! I sir?

CARRAVAGIO Yes.

FERDINANDO Did she say aught of me?

CARRAVAGIO Thou hast a masterly command of feature.
But there is fear and trouble in thine eye.
'Tis not contrition. No: and a wild hope
Gleams now and then upon thy troubled fear;
Like glimpsing sunshine on the wint'ry waves.
What mischief hast thou done?

FERDINANDO Mischief! What I?

CARRAVAGIO What hast thou done that yet may be conceal'd?

FERDINANDO You much amaze me, sir, by what you say.

CARRAVAGIO I am but in this house, professional;
Nor does it suit my nature thus to pry.
But thou hast done, or I mistake my trade,
Some guilty deed, that flatters thee with hope.

ACT I, Scene IX

FERDINANDO.

How should this cunning artist thus detect?
He and Teresa have conferr'd together.
The countess too has something said of me.
Are they in league? Can she have made disclosure?
And yet, me-thinks she would not well do that.
I told Teresa, I was in the room.
If I, why not another? I am safe!
I will Teresa's thoughts so turn aslant,

That the suspicion shall remove from me.
Had but the countess been a little shrewd.
'Tis true she took me for the count.—What then?
She may again accept me, for myself;
At least, 'tis best, I think, still to remain.

ACT I, Scene X

TERESA *and* FERDINANDO.

TERESA What, Ferdinando! wherefore are you here?
Not gone to Florence, nor with Carravagio?

FERDINANDO I do not like that painter in this house.

TERESA No, Ferdinando!

FERDINANDO No. How does my lady?

TERESA Dejected; thoughtful; speaking not a word.

FERDINANDO If we were in some safe and secret place,
I would, Teresa, something say to you.—
But is my lady very sad indeed?

TERESA Have I not told you, almost wildly sad?

FERDINANDO She spoke with Carravagio, as I know.

TERESA She did. What of it; passing to her room?

FERDINANDO Were you no present when she spoke with him?

TERESA 'Twas but a word or two, and quickly said.

FERDINANDO But what she said, you cannot truly tell?

TERESA Indeed, not I.

FERDINANDO Teresa.—

TERESA Well?

FERDINANDO Teresa;
You are a woman, knowing and observant.
I wish we were in some secluded room;
Where no intrusion might break in upon us.—
How did the painter look when you saw him?

TERESA He pitied much the countess.

FERDINANDO Pitied!
These artists sure, are men of subtile craft.
He pitied?

TERESA Ay!

FERDINANDO What did he know to pity?
I went last night into our lady's room.—

TERESA You told me so;—a daring shame it was.

FERDINANDO Well; have you learnt though, if she heard me speak?

TERESA I did.

FERDINANDO What said she?
Lookt like one that kens[34]
Dread things, invisible to mortal sight.—
Just like Paulina in the picture there,
When told her love was not the God Anubis,[35]
Pale agonized, almost foregone in mind.

---

34 An archaic word meaning "knows".
35 Anubis was the ancient Egyptian god of death, the afterlife, tombs, depicted as a man with the head of a jackal.

FERDINANDO Think you the painter knows that I was there?
It may be good for him to turn on me.
This is a matter that cannot long hide:
Let you and I, Teresa, council keep;—
Have all our eyes and all our ears set open.
These men of art do other things at night,
Than watch the moon-light as it, brightening, falls
On busts and statues in a gallery.

ACT I, Scene XI

TERESA.

'Tis plain, 'tis sure she grieves not for her lord.
My thoughts and fears fell first on Ferdinando;
He is of that complexion, and so bold;
And I have seen him gaze profanely at her.
But Carravagio! True he eyes her oft;
And in his study, here and there are seen,
Both nymphs and goddesses, where one may trace
Her comely lineaments; yet in his gaze,
He looks not as a man on woman looks,
But as a student pond'ring o'er a text.
I should as soon expect to find him bedded
With Venus or Diana, as with her.
Lo, where she comes, dejected and perplext.

ACT I, Scene XII

ANTONIA *and* TERESA.[36]

ANTONIA My lord, you said, was to be here at noon.

TERESA So Ferdinando told me. Heard you not
What he reported when he came last night?

---

36 The 1812 edition does not list the actors for this scene; these have been restored here.

ANTONIA Eternal horror blot the fatal night.
I heard him not; I was wrapt up in sleep.
Oh! my lov'd lord, that could so rashly leave
Thy faithful wife defenceless while a slave.—
Where is the fiend?—

TERESA Whom, my dear lady, whom?

ANTONIA The sacrilegious and infernal snake
That crawled, unheard, to—

TERESA Ferdinando?

ANTONIA—Yes.

TERESA You heard him then when he was in the room?

ANTONIA Darest thou, presumptuous wench, say that I knew?

TERESA Pardon me, madam, if I say amiss.
It was, indeed, an impious intrusion.

ANTONIA Ha! how intrusion? What know'st thou of it?

TERESA Was he not seen by signor Carravagio?
He often walks the gallery at night.

ANTONIA Go send the painter, instantly, to me.

TERESA Here is a riddle, ravell'd and perplext!

ACT I, Scene XIII

ANTONIA.

If I could 'raze conviction from my mind,
And think of all as an unhappy dream.—

But if all know it, surely there is proof;
And the poor victim of perfidious sleep,
Shall be blasphem'd by all the lib'lous world:
Nor will the cloister'd burial avail.

ACT, Scene XIV

CARRAVAGIO *and* ANTONIA.

CARRAVAGIO I wait obedient, lady, to your will.

ANTONIA It is not, Carravagio, wise of you,
To walk and pry about the house at night.

CARRAVAGIO Some one has slandered me, to say I pry.
Save in the gall'ry, when the moon is up,
Or in the porticos, to study shadows,[37]
I never quit my chamber after dark.

ANTONIA Why were you in the gallery last night?
The moon was down before I went to sleep,
And it was pitchy dark;—a dismal night!

CARRAVAGIO My honour'd lady, credit not this tale.
I had retired before eleven rung.
If there were pryers in the gallery,
I was not one. I never will betray.

ANTONIA Betray! What sir would you betray of mine?

CARRAVAGIO Pardon the word.

ANTONIA Sir, you may now retire.

---

37 The Errata corrects this from "porticos".

ACT I, Scene XV

ANTONIA.

He never will betray! Does he then know?
He went to bed before eleven rung.—
How could he know, to say he'll not betray?
He went to bed, but he might rise again;
And he is wont to walk about at night.
Triple confusion was the villain him?
Ha! Ferdinando! I will sift him next.

ACT I, Scene XVI

ANTONIA *and* FERDINANDO.

ANTONIA How dar'd you, wretch! break, at the dead of night,
Into my chamber as I sleeping lay?

FERDINANDO Was there no other there?

ANTONIA Great God! what other?

FERDINANDO Madam, 'tis true I found your door unbarr'd;
Enter'd unheard, as—

ANTONIA Wretch! you shall be torn
To rags by tygers, when my lord returns.
I could, myself, rive thy accursed flesh.—
Oh! Heav'n!—Oh! Heav'n!—to leave me so forlorn.

FERDINANDO (*I'll brave her out.*)—Have confidence in me.
But when you next in this intrigue indulge,
Dismiss him ere you sleep.

ANTONIA Whom! whom! accurst?

FERDINANDO He that usurp'd the linen of my lord;
For had it been the count himself that came.—
But trust to me. If you are calm and wise,
I'll be as secret as your paramour.

ANTONIA Hence! hence! insulting traitor; hence! I say.

ACT I, Scene XVI

ANTONIA.

Was it not him? 'Twas Carravagio then:
Yet he has ever seem'd to me respectful;
And by the enthusiasm of his art,
Wholly enchanted. This detested fox
Wears an audacious smile, which more than once,
Has, with a terrible presage, alarm'd me.
Yet Carravagio too said I was safe,
For he would not betray.—Both know it then.
But which?—Who is the guilty thief of me?
Whom shall I charge to my belov'd Urbano?
And will he credit me? Alas! alas!
I must no longer claim him for my lord.
Yet, have I never felt one swerving thought
From the pure tenour of my marriage vow,
But ever been in my allegiance faithful.
Faithful!—O God! am I a faithless wife?
I, who so hop'd in lofty pride of mind,
To show out sensual italian dames,
That Portia, nor the mother of the Grachii,
Were fictions feign'd. Oh! what have I become?
Sunk to a level with the pronest vile,
And most abhorrent to my wretched self.

ACT II, Scene I

CARRAVAGIO.

I cannot bend my thoughts upon my work; Nor dare I note what fancy would suggest. What can it be?—She has sustain'd a wrong, Which dyes her face alternately with shame, And bleaches with disgust. Alas! poor lady.

ACT II, Scene II

TERESA *and* CARRAVAGIO.

TERESA How! here again! Whom seek you, signor, here?
You were not wont to walk in this saloon?

CARRAVAGIO This morning, Ferdinando has affairs,
And I am otherwise not very well.

TERESA Not very well?

CARRAVAGIO Ay! Why should that surprise you?

TERESA You walk too much, good signor, in the night.
Night is the season for refreshing sleep,
And those who trespass on its lonely hours,
Have cares, or fears, or troubled thoughts, or love?

CARRAVAGIO You speak oracular. My art requires
That I should mark the various falling light;
And who can see the moon-beam, or the lamp,
Shed their true bright'ning, but when night prevails.[38]

TERESA Cannot you be content with sun-shine hues?
They charm the eye with more variety.

---

38 It is noteworthy that the real painter Caravaggio (Michelangelo Merisi da Caravaggio: 1571-1610) was interested in dramatic lighting via candles at night, called *chiaroscuro*.

CARRAVAGIO It is my taste,—my genius prompts me so.

TERESA Pray what is that? What is this genius, sir?
I hear of it, yet know not what it is.

CARRAVAGIO 'Tis some peculiarity of mood,
Which makes the difference between mind and mind,
That figure, feature, colour, gait and air,
Make between man and man.—From sense it comes.

TERESA How may that be? We feel, taste, hear, and smell;
And saving accidents, see things alike?

CARRAVAGIO True! but the working is unknown to me.

TERESA I understand: some have a keener relish
Of this or that, more than their neighbours have.

CARRAVAGIO 'Tis so, I think. Some by the ear, are charm'd
With plaintive melodies, or cheerful sounds;
Some by the eye, with various forms and hues.
The senses are the portals of the mind;
And genius enters by the most frequented,
Or that which nature has constructed best.

TERESA Genius then makes, if I conceive aright,
By practice, or some liveliness of sense,
Men prone to find, and seize their means of pleasure;
And as you oft foregoe the midnight sleep,
To catch the shadows of the moony hour,
Or rise in company, as I have seen you,
Regardless of all decorous demeanour, T
o bid a stranger beauty bend aslant;
Some other, by his different genius led,
Would seize on chance, nor fear he might offend.

CARRAVAGIO You're wond'rous metaphysical Teresa!—
But why so suddenly at odds in thought?

TERESA The moon, I think, went down at ten last night;
Nor were there any lights for you at two.—
How came you to be stirring at tat hour?

CARRAVAGIO I! I Teresa? Wherefore ask you this?
Your lady chided me, and said I pry.
What has been done? What ill is thought of me?

TERESA It was at two that Ferdinando came.

CARRAVAGIO Well?

TERESA Saw you him not?

CARRAVAGIO At two last night, I?
I heard eleven strike when in my bed,
And slumb'ring soon, waked not before the dawn.

TERESA Was ever robb'ry more atrocious done?

CARRAVAGIO Robb'ry! am I suspected of a theft?

TERESA O no, no, no; it was not done by you.
Oh! my sweet lady to be plunder'd so!
How will her lov'd and loving lord deplore!

ACT II, Scene III

CARRAVAGIO *and* FERDINANDO.

CARRAVAGIO 'Tis very strange! How could they doubt of me?
Why should a robb'ry crimson her with shame?
Ferdinando!—

FERDINANDO Sir! well?

CARRAVAGIO (*I am distrest.*)

FERDINANDO If you don't want me, sir, I may retire.

CARRAVAGIO Was it at two, that you came home last night?

FERDINANDO It was: Pray what is it to you? Am I
Bound to inform you of my coming home;
Or when, or how, I spend my master's time?

CARRAVAGIO Friend, be not insolent. Know, sullen knave,
That not thy master would so answer me.

FERDINANDO No: were he wise, he would not use his tongue.

CARRAVAGIO For this time I can pass thy insolence.—
There has been done a fatal deed last night.

FERDINANDO I know there has; and do you, sir, blame me?

CARRAVAGIO Art thou afraid I should, ill-manner'd cur?
But if in matter so juridical,
I could persuade the world of my skill,
There would not want sufficient evidence,
The forehead mark of guilt is set so plain.

FERDINANDO Shall I be ruin'd by your painting fancies?
What is there, sir, in this same pencil craft,
To make of me a villain or a saint,
But the devices of a plotting brain?

CARRAVAGIO Think'st thou, lewd epicure, thy sensual eye
Can the fine workings of the mind discern,
As they develope to the painter's sight;
Or that my art but ministers to pomp,

And has no influence in that holy process,
Which separates the pure celestial mind,
From such vile carnal dross, as rules in thee?
The painter's pencil, in expression true,
Conveys a moral like the poet's pen;
And feelings faithful on the easel limm'd,
Instruct the spirit and improve the heart,
Like eloquence, with all the shades of phrase,
Or poetry, embodied on the stage.
Go; fear my skill; and if thou can'st, atone;
For thou hast done that which I dread to think.—
A deed so dark, leads to a deadly sequel.

ACT II, Scene IV

TERESA *and* FERDINANDO.

TERESA Stop! traitor, stop! or if there be a name
Of more perfidious villany expressive,
I'll call thee that, incarnated of Hell!

FERDINANDO What means the woman with this noisy riot

TERESA Thou smooth unfathomable villany,
To vent the dev'lish venom of thy guile,
With such insidious plausibility
Against an honest and unworldly man!

FERDINANDO Think you, the painter then is innocent?
Think you that one so skill'd in trimming hues,
Is yet so little practiced in his craft
As not to make his visage for the time?—
I've been the valet of our lord the count,
Ten years and more; and he is but a stranger:
In all that time, what ill know you of me;
What good of him?

TERESA I know that you have been
A flagrant master of my silly sex,
While he has but a mastership attain'd
In forms and shades: spare fruit of patient study.

FERDINANDO How should he know of what was done last night?
Answer me that. What spirit serves his ear,
To give advertisement of secret things?
Grant him the skill to spy into our thoughts;
'Tis but the present thought that rules the face;
Still as it shifts, a different guize succeeds;
How then should he know of an act that's past?
He could as well tell when you went to sleep
As know this secret, had he not been told.
Was he a witness, or a party, think you?
But what, Teresa, does the countess say?

TERESA She sits disconsolate, and only sighs,
Or starts, as 'twere, by sudden anguish stung;
And frantic flutt'ring, flies from room to room.

FERDINANDO When was't she told you what had pass'd?

TERESA Told me!
She never told me.

FERDINANDO No! How knew you then?

TERESA I guess'd of something dismal by her grief,
And when you told me you were in the room.—
Why do you beat upon your brow so fiercely?

FERDINANDO Did she not send you to enquire?

TERESA Not she.

FERDINANDO Why stir you then so busily in it?

TERESA Think you that such a thing should chance, and I
Not seek to learn the truth and circumstance.

FERDINANDO We are, Teresa, but a pair of fools.
In all this, there may be but our conception.
Sift you herself—'tis meet she should be vext,—
That such as I broke in upon her sleep.

TERESA But how came you to think of Carravagio?

FERDINANDO I learnt from you what had, or may have, chanc'd,
And knowing his nocturnal rambles thought—

TERESA You turn my fancy, fellow, all awry;
I may be wrong, and yield to false conceits,
Or thou art but a deep and deeper knave.

ACT II, Scene V

FERDINANDO.

I have o'er-leap'd myself. Had I not told This curious lynx of being in the room,
The countess still, perhaps, had nothing said. Lo where she comes!—I'll stand apart and spy.

ACT II, Scene VI

ANTONIA *and* FERDINANDO.

ANTONIA Let me no longer bend to this despair;
While I exhaust myself, with useless passion,
The secret Tarquin may escape secure.
Shame that restrains the speaking of my wrong,
Is, in this case, the minister of guilt.—
What though I may to cloister'd sorrow go,
Who will believe my chastity of mind,
If I depart and leave the spoiler free?—

Let me be calm and patient to discover
Which by the loathsome Belial is possess'd.
Why should I doubt? But still the fiend denies
And speaks as if he saw!—Peace, peace my heart;
'Tis done, 'tis done—nor sighs nor tears avail.
No sigh can turn the moment wafted by;
Nor tear obliviate the guilty stain.—
How my brain kindles when this wretch appears—
Ferdinando!—

FERDINANDO Madam!—

ANTONIA Hither; art there?

FERDINANDO (*She overawes me!—what can ye intend?*)

ANTONIA How dar'd you violate?—O God! O God!
And must I stoop to speak on such a theme?
What devil tempted you into my room?
No more prevarication; well you know
There was no other, but yourself, with me.

FERDINANDO You knew me then?

ANTONIA Say not, hell-fox, I knew.

FERDINANDO Softly, sweet lady, be a little wise,
No one may know if we are shrewd ourselves;
'Tis true you knew me not. But now—she's mad!

ACT II, Scene VII

FERDINANDO.

This flaming rage is female artifice.
Had I not told Teresa all was safe—[39]

---

39 The 1812 publication has "fafe".

Had I suppress'd that I was in the room,A
nd sent the mouser prying through the house,
All had gone well.—Curse on my cautious fear:
My rash precaution has betray'd the whole.

ACT II, Scene VIII

CARRAVAGIO, TERESA, *and* FERDINANDO.

CARRAVAGIO Ha! Ferdinando! friend, art thou discover'd?
TERESA At length together I have found them both.—
Stay Ferdinando, for I come to speak,
And face to face bring out the dismal truth.

FERDINANDO Who gave you right?

TERESA Who gave me right!

FERDINANDO Ay, who?

TERESA Shall deeds of such opprobrious act be done,
And no one dare to search how, or by whom!

CARRAVAGIO Humanity, thou firm complexion'd bronze,
Commissions her. Such misery and woe,
As wring the spirit of her hapless lady,
Dictate authority to all that's human.—
I met the countess flying as I came,
Her face distorted, and her fingers spread,
And all her figure shrunken, like one sick,
Seiz'd with the loathe of some detested drug.

FERDINANDO Good signor Carravagio hear my reason.—
This is a matter that involves us all;
Or you, who trespass on untimely hours;
Or wise Teresa here, who serves the countess;
Or I, whom accident brought home so late;

Must first sustain the charge of this great wrong.
It is not fit that we should meddle in't.—
We are not well in circumstances suited.
Each may some truth know in a different way.
And that which each of us apart suspects,
May be as different as we are ourselves.
Wait till the count return; then let us speak.
Teresa's fancy runs on midnight rape;
And you, sir, think, perchance, of robbery;
While I who found the door unbarr'd and entered.—

CARRAVAGIO Went you into your lady's room last night?

TERESA He did, he did, good signor Carravagio!

FERDINANDO Do I deny?—

CARRAVAGIO   Horrible satyr! cease.
The midnight vision of thee in her chamber,
Had been enough to redden ruby-red,
The diamond purity of such a mind.
Oh! noble lady, virtuous in vain!

FERDINANDO Did I not say that he would turn on me?

TERESA If he be false, how shall the true be known?
If thou art true, what shape takes villany?

FERDINANDO Think you, or you Teresa, or your dame,
To daunt me down by this conspiracy?
It is not, sir, in nature credible,
That a poor menial should unwelcom'd climb,
And love licentious where he dar'd not look.
Guard well yourself good signor Carravagio;
We know your practice at the midnight hour.

ACT II, Scene IX

CARRAVAGIO *and* TERESA.

CARRAVAGIO Let us, Teresa, summon up the house;
Send for the count, and, with some speedy justice,
Avenge this matchless sacrilegious sin.

TERESA As yet my lady, sir, has not complain'd:
'Tis true we have her tears and sorrow seen;
But still we know not well what has been done;—
She may be vex'd and yet not greatly rue.

CARRAVAGIO You do her wrong, you do her wrong, Teresa.
To such a lofty and majestic mind,
The very utt'rance of her direful taint,
Will be as when the soul forsakes the frame.

TERESA See where she comes!
CARRAVAGIO How solemn and august!
Like Juno stepping from the throne of Jove.

ACT II, Scene X

ANTONIA, CARRAVAGIO, *and* TERESA.

ANTONIA Good Carravagio, by your leave a moment,—I
would converse with her a little space.
I pray you, Carravagio, for the day
To take command of this ill-fated mansion.
Place special sentinels at all the gates:
Men you can trust. Look well I pray you, signor,
That no one fly; nor least of all that fiend—
See Carravagio, Ferdinando fly not.
And, if you will, send for the count my lord—
Good Carravagio it will be too late.
He will be here;—he will come soon enough!

CARRAVAGIO Alas! alas!

ACT II, Scene XI

ANTONIA *and* TERESA.

ANTONIA Why does he weep, Teresa?

TERESA Sad fears and bodements hang on all our minds,
And wilder fancies overcome our thoughts,
Than the grim night-mare brings in troubl'd dreams.

ANTONIA Last night, Teresa, as I lay asleep,
Methought my noble lord, the Count Urbano,
The Count Urbano, my dear wedded lord,
Came in unheard, and softly sought my couch;
But when I woke before the dawn of day,
I was alone, and sinking back in sleep,
Dreamt that the devil had usurp'd my breast.
The fearful image startled me awake;
And, clearing swift the hazy drouze that still
Hung like a vapour on my faculties,
I has persuasion horrible of things
Which have infected me with desp'rate death.

TERESA Oh my dear lady!—Oh! alas! alas!

ANTONIA But still bright Hope rose like the hectic bloom,
That tints the cheek of a consuming fair;
And spite of conscious sense beguil'd my wish,
Till I had learnt who had profan'd my room.
Then like the flame that burst upon the sight
Of wretched Hecuba, when she unclos'd
Her window on the final night of Troy,
The hideous certainty shone full upon me,
And show'd the ruin and the sack atchiev'd.

TERESA Oh devilish serpent that could so invade
The hallow'd Eden of your wedded faith!

ACT III, Scene I

CARRAVAGIO *and* TERESA.

CARRAVAGIO The priest has left her: I saw him depart;
He look'd behind just as he left the gate,
And, crossing, heavenward turn'd his eyes and sighed.

TERESA May I go in, and ask her how she does?

CARRAVAGIO No: patient wait, and leave her till she call.
'Tis impious to pass with curious eye,
Into the sanctu'ry of hopeless sorrow.

TERESA Have you sent messengers to bring the count?

CARRAVAGIO Not yet, Teresa.

TERESA Heavens! why not yet,
When such an hideous outrage has been done?

CARRAVAGIO Peace, peace. What has been done, can he undo?

TERESA But when do you intend to call him home?

CARRAVAGIO Not till the guilty has confession made, To the
content of all th' assembled household,
That she was innocent, and knew him not;
Or till she has decided on her doom.

TERESA What mean you, sir? Has she not told us both
That she, to-night, would in the convent lie?

CARRAVAGIO But whether as a nun, or with the dead?

TERESA You chill my blood. She will not slay herself?

CARRAVAGIO She had in thought, before the friar came,
An awful enterprize.

TERESA How knew you that?

CARRAVAGIO I saw the index written on her brow.

TERESA We should not, sir, then leave her long alone.

CARRAVAGIO Woman; restrain this eagerness to pry;
Nor with thy pert and seamstress pity, vex
Her solemn magnanimity. Know'st thou
That there are minds of such pure element,
That the alloy'd and current of the world,
Have little common with them but the name;
And hers is of that kind.

TERESA But Ferdinando.
How do you mean, sir, to proceed with him?
It is not right to leave him ranging free.—

CARRAVAGIO While doubtful of his fate, his mind may change:
He is perplext. To his material soul,
The tragic issue of his flagrant daring, Is as a new creation.
Men like him, Cannot, in their sublimest fancies, guess
The moods and motives of superior minds.

TERESA Why lay such stress, sir, upon his confession?
Do you believe the countess was to blame?

CARRAVAGIO No, woman, no: I never thought the thought;
But fame and reputation stand with her
Next in degree to virtue: for the least,
The sacrifice of life were cheap to her.
Did he confess, and place her honour clear,

Her virtue yet might lift her from the soil,
And make her shine the opal of the land.

TERESA But where's the need, when we are so convinced,
To place such consequence to his confession?
We may console her if we tell her so.

CARRAVAGIO We never can.—Pray thee think less of us.—
Those that but know the palpable of men,
And such compose the throng and crowd of life,
Judge by the fact, and place all in one class,
On whom the law bestows a common name.
She has confess'd adult'ry! Who will pause
To learn the circumstances, nor class her down
With those free wantons, whose lewd highway riots,
Have chang'd the brazen of the lawyer's front,
To blushing copper in th' examination.
But good Teresa, let us quit the theme;
My heart is full, and swelling to distress.
Alas! how little in this world of things,
Are held, the feelings that pervade the heart.
All that high honour and bright recompence
Which should inspire us, and make sweet our toil,
Come by the Alchymy of have and want,
In the post obit value of our works!

ACT III, Scene II

TERESA, ANTONIO, *and* CARRAVAGIO.

TERESA Signor, the countess comes.

ANTONIA—Well, Carravagio;
Have you, in all things, done as I desired?

CARRAVAGIO I have, my honoured lady,—all—

TERESA But one:
He has not yet sent for, my lord, the count.

ANTONIA In that omission, he has judged well.—
I thank you, Carravagio: it was wise.

TERESA Nor Ferdinando has he yet arrested.

ANTONIA Teresa, doubtless he considers well.—
You may retire apart: when there is need,
I will require your presence; but till then—Teresa?—
Go, and lay prepared for me, The dress of simple white.

TERESA Which, my dear lady?

ANTONIA That which I wore when I became a bride.

ACT III, Scene III

ANTONIA *and* CARRAVAGIO.

ANTONIA My worthy friend, why falls this shower of sorrow?
What we, afflictions and mischances deem,
Are but the movements of that viewless chain,
On which, dependant from the throne of Heaven,
Hang all inferior and created things.
Nought from the vassalage of fate is free,
But Virtue: she alone exemption boasts,
And in her own allodian grandeur firm,[40]
Denies the claims that Chance and Time pretend.
What! though this fabric crumble into dust,
And with the sentenc'd globe return again
Into the elements, and all to nothing;
That which is I, shall purified ascend,

---

[40] Presumably Galt is referring here to "Allodial title"—ownership of real property independent of any superior landlord, in other words, independent wealth.

And with the general vanishing of things,
Behold its dross and blemish pass away.
But come, 'tis fit we should proceed to trial.
Good signor, call the household to attend,
And such esteemed and venerated neighbours,
As by their testimony, may avouch
The high result of what shall come to pass.

CARRAVAGIO It is then meet the culprit should attend.

ANTONIA Undoubtedly. How! think you otherwise?

CARRAVAGIO No, gracious lady; but I feared, the sight
Might wake afresh the anguish of your mind.

ANTONIA Good, worthy, Carravagio, that is past;
The struggle done and vanquish'd Shame laid low.
Who is there fashioned in corporeal form,
That I may not with steady eye survey?
Yea not the taunt of my own true-lov'd lord
In giving credence to the menial's tale,
Would disconcert my all-collected mind.

CARRAVAGIO Is it your pleasure that the count should come?

ANTONIA No, spare me that—I could not bear his grief,
Nor part from him without a painful pang.—
I pray you, friend, be speedy in this task;
For idle time is like a giant's robe,
It loads, perplexes, and exhausts the strength.

ACT III, Scene IV

CARRAVAGIO.

She has decided as I thought she would. Alas! alas! but who may dare to thwart The high resolves of such a soul as hers.

ACT III, Scene V

TERESA *and* CARRAVAGIO.

TERESA Where is the countess gone?—All is prepar'd.

CARRAVAGIO Attend you here, and what she may require
Give without speaking, and with lowly service,
Such as befits our mean and abject natures,
When call'd to offices of awful issue.

TERESA How is she now?

CARRAVAGIO Magnificent! sublime!
Like the archangel on the wall of Heav'n,
Who looking down on our sublunar orb,
Computes the good and ill of human life,
And finds a vast preponderance of ill.

ACT III, Scene VI

TERESA.

Ah me! that one so fair should fall so foul!
Betray'd unconsciously. She has resolv'd,
To quit the world and pine away a nun:
Doom'd by the crime of Fortune to a jail.—

ACT III, Scene VII

TERESA *and* FERDINANDO.

TERESA Well Ferdinando, this is joyous work;
Thou art in truth a special gay gallant.

FERDINANDO   To you nor other, will I answer give,
Till face to face with witnesses we meet.—

So! he has sent to call the neighbours in;
And summons up the servants to a show.
Ay, let him call and summon as he may;
The world shall learn who was, or which, to blame.
'Tis shrewd of him, that I must needs admit,
To turn on me and bait me for the scorn.
But fraud is fraud; this will not last them long—
The shallow silvering will soon be bare,
And all the base and counterfeit reveal'd.

TERESA You then persist in your innocence?

FERDINANDO I do, and will do, till they shew such proof
As hands may touch, and eyes may look upon.
I am not made so ductile as they deem.

TERESA Behold the neighbours and the servants come,
With tearful eyes and faces full of woe;
And Carravagio sadder than them all.

ACT III, Scene VIII

CARRAVAGIO, TERESA, FERDINANDO, &c.

CARRAVAGIO Good friends, by order of our noble lady,
You are assembl'd for a solemn cause.
This house so long, the honour of the land,
Renown'd for hospitality and all
The liberal virtues that should wait on rank,
Has been the scene of a tremendous outrage.
Beneath the masque of darkness, in the guise
Of wedded Confidence, dire Rape last night
Stole in and rifled with opprobrious daring
The chaste embraces of our lady's love.
Th' infernal robber undetected fled;—
But various circumstance, of pointing proof,
Has fix'd the guilty charge on Ferdinando.
For bearing late commission from our lord

He did presume—Oh impious presumption!
To slip the door and glide into her room,
Unheard, unseen, as she defenceless lay,
All in the dark and negligence of sleep.
On this great fact the countess builds her charge—
But lo she comes!—make way—apart—divide.
What mighty grandeur in her form dilates
Beyond the comprehension of our thoughts!

ACT III, Scene IX

ANTONIA, CARRAVAGIO, TERESA, FERDINANDO, &c.

ANTONIA Have you disclosed to them what has mischanced?

CARRAVAGIO I have performed all to the point commanded;
Would you that I should still proceed in it?

ANTONIA It might for delicacy be as well—
But no: I will myself. My worthy friends,
In common wrongs, such as may fall on all,
We may entrust the agency of others;
And purchas'd advocacy may avail.
But in my dire unprecedented case,
I should impair my own preserv'd esteem,
Preserv'd unspotted in th' unconscious sin,
Could I forego my painful vindication, Ferdinando.—

FERDINANDO Madam.—

ANTONIA Do you confess?

FERDINANDO That I did pass into your room, I do;
That I know well my lord was wrong'd last night,
I also must declare.

TERESA To me he said,
That when he entered he believed you knew

ANTONIA When the time comes to ask for your report,
Then tell your knowledge.—Yes, I know full well
That in the world the guilt will so be thought.—
Do you confess?

FERDINANDO How! that I did the wrong?

CARRAVAGIO Out with the quibble, sir—out with it all.
I see it working in thy alt'ring visage.

ANTONIO Let him proceed.—what though he dare pretend
That in the crime the blame must rest on me,
I but desire confession of the fact.
Do you confess?—Still blush you to atone?

CARRAVAGIO Give way, give way, O miserable man!
To the contrition that begins to rise.

ANTONIA Turn, turn, O turn thee from thy fatal lapse,
And strive to reach the upward tract again.
The path of vice lies with inviting slope
Down the declivity; and every step
Is smoother, easier, lower still and lower,
Till nothing from the headlong fall can save.
In mercy to thyself confession make.

TERESA The fiercest tortures, penal craft employs,
To wrench out secrets from the clenched knave,
Will tear the truth from thy obdurate breast.

ANTONIA Patience, Teresa, cherish milder thoughts,
And e'en in injury benev'lence own.
Benevolence is like the glorious sun,
Whose free impartial splendour fosters all:
It is the radiance of the human soul,
The proof and sign of its celestial birth.
All other creatures of corporeal ore,

Partake the common qualities of man:
Love, hatred, anger, all particular aims!
But in this infinite and pure effusion,
This only passion of divinity,
He grows the rival of the heav'nly God.—
Do you confess?

FERDINANDO What is't I should confess?—
What is this sin, this robbery, this wrong?
Where is the loss? Where is the detriment?
When theft is wrought a certain void is left;
When malice strikes, a wound or blain appears;
Wrong ever comes in manifest effect;
But this is fantasy, or falsely charged.

ANTONIA Behold, thou shrewd equivocating fiend, T
he test thou dar'st desire—

TERESA Oh! horror! horror! She has stabb'd herself!—

ANTONIA Wilt thou yet confess?

TERESA Help! help!—fly all ye wond'ring—

ANTONIA Silence, woman;
Attend thy duty, and support me here.
This is no time for idle exclamation.—
I want but yet the pleasure ere I die,
To hear him say he uninvited came.
But if too rapid, ebb my streaming life,
May this dread act, my only sure appeal,
Deter the sullying Slander from my fame.

TERESA See how the sheety pale of death appears,
On that bright face that tempted thee to sin.
ANTONIA Woman, forbear; nor once again presume
To breathe allusion to the fatal theme.—
Think you he will confess?

CARRAVAGIO I think he will.

ANTONIA Would he were speedy, for I faint apace.
My eyes grow dim—God bless you, worthy friends.
Commend me, signor, to my dearest lord.

TERESA Alas! alas! she dies!—

CARRAVAGIO It is away!—Her pure and heav'nly spirit is away.
Oh! it has flown like a poor frighten'd bird,
Appealing to the Heavens against the hand
That plunder'd ruthlessly its early nest.—
Friends, let us quit this theatre of blood,
With the sad moral graven on our hearts.
One guilty act is parent to a race;
And the last born still more detestable,
In bent and form than all that did precede.

TERESA What would'st thou with the knife? Its sheath of blood,
Wert thou a man of human mould compos'd,
Would be like mortal pestilence to thee.

CARRAVAGIO Rouse thee, poor wretch! from thy
astonishment; There is no visionary horror here.
The fatal steel in thy amazed sight,
So dropping rubies is no magic fiction;
Nor this fair casket, that so late contained
A glorious gem by Heav'ns own master placed,
A dreamy show; but all reality.—
Tortures await thee.—

FERDINANDO Thus from them I fly.

———

END.

CLYTEMNESTRA, A Tragedy

Characters.

ORESTES
PYLADES
EGYSTHUS

CLYTEMNESTRA

The stage represents an open space near the Palace, and the Temple of Phoebus in Argos.

ACT I, Scene I

ORESTES.

Now has the great predestined day arriv'd,
When by thy aid, O ever-radiant Phoebus,
Orestes must his destiny fulfil.
Tremendous destiny! that gives my hand
The matricidal knife!—Make firm my heart,
And to th' avenging of my father's death,
On her that bore me, grant such note and fame

To the dread act, that never guilt again,
Like Clytemnestra's, may surprize the world.
O Agamemnon! my heroic sire!
Could not the charm of thy atchiev'd renown
Restrain th' adultress!—Scarce from Troy return'd,
To be so murder'd,—and myself, poor babe!
To clear the kingdom for the lewd Egysthus,
Before my birth was sentenced to be slain,
But by the nurse who had my father rear'd,
Sav'd; and while yet unswaddled, sent by night
To my sad uncle's court. His kindly care
Bred me to manhood; but the Gods convinc'd
My early youth that they had work for me.
Blood will have blood. My father's claims the blow,
And my own wrongs extenuate the deed.

ACT I, Scene II

ORESTES *and* PYLADES.

ORESTES Well, my Pylades, have you seen my sister?
How does she fare in the maternal brothel?

PYLADES As a bright jewel among offal cast,
Her native purity remains unchang'd.
She lives apart a pious pensive life,
And weeps unheard her guilty mother's sin.

ORESTES And what of her, and the abhorr'd Egysthus?

PYLADES Rather than ask, imagine. Nothing chang'd
Is the wild flame of Clytemnestra's passion;
Though every day th' opprobrious paramour,
Insulting nature might provoke her scorn.

ORESTES And does my sister but bewail the guilt?
A loftier spirit better would become,
Atrides issue and exalted blood.

PYLADES But gentle is the fair Electra's soul,
And in her bosom, full of heavy sorrow,
The vex of indignation never stirs.—
Her meek and unrepining spirit shows
A holy brightness in its clouded sphere;
Like the pale moon that on the vapoury earth,
Sheds without heat the pure celestial light.

ORESTES Methinks I should have more courageous felt,
Did she possess the temper of revenge
To urge me if I shrunk.

PYLADES Have I not sworn
To bear my part, in this just enterprize,
Against Egysthus?

ORESTES—But high fate ordains
A greater act; and Agamemnon's shade
Demands a sacrifice to match his death.

PYLADES What mean you?

ORESTES—Justice.

PYLADES How!

ORESTES Full retribution.

PYLADES On whom?

ORESTES The guilty.

PYLADES What! your mother?

ORESTES Yes.—
Why turn you pale and look on me so strange?
I am Orestes! Agamemnon's son!

With him th' immortal halo first was thrown,
Around the helmed head of bloody war;
And men, up-rising from their sordid aims,
Were taught that wounds, yea death itself was gain,
When found in battle fought but for renown.
The unborn races of the utmost times,
The last circumf'rence of posterity,
Will sound applause to Agamemnon's name.
But he, with all his glory in its noon,
Was, by the demon of accurst desire,
Torn from his sphere, and like a falling star,
Extinguish'd in the world's astonish'd gaze;
And should not such a crime be all reveng'd?

PYLADES Think, Clytemnestra is your mother,—think.

ORESTES But justice no propinquity respects;
And fate, by all the tenour of my life,
Has shown me fashion'd for a solemn end.
Know! Heav'n at times sends forth predestined men
To stir the world, and from the sensual foul
To cleanse th' immortal element of thought.
Of such were Hercules and Theseus.
What toils they bore to rid the earth o'errun,
With hideous offspring of perverted passion!
My conscious spirit claims to rank itself
With their high phalanx, and by some great act
To give an epocha to history;
That sages wond'ring o'er the past may say,
"Such was the world before Orestes' time;
But his high-aim'd atchievement changing all;
Crimes, bold and catching once, like strange diseases,
Grew mild and vanish'd from the frame of man."

PYLADES Sublime! Incomprehensible! This strange
And warm enthusiasm that pervades
Thy lofty spirit, has transform'd thy nature,

Lighting a purpose dark and terrible,
With such a flame of holy charity,
That I am aw'd, and tremble at thy virtue.
Thou art no more, Orestes! he with whom
My youthful pastimes were so gaily spent!
But I have sworn to be as true to this,
In his great business, as his own right hand.—
Lo, where your sister, fair Electra comes.

ACT I, Scene III

ELECTRA, ORESTES *and* PYLADES.

ELECTRA My noble brother—

ORESTES Rise, Electra, rise:
Too long the daughter of the king of heroes,
Has bent in lowliness and pined forlorn.
Why knelt you thus to me?

ELECTRA Your mein,

Orestes, O'erawes my spirit; and my heart foregone,
The joyous throb with which I sought you here,
Stands in my bosom, fearful and restrained,
As if I saw, incarnated in you,
The energy of an avenging God.
But wherefore here, at this most perilous hour?
This is the portico of Phoebus' temple.—

ORESTES Hail holy temple of my guardian God!

ELECTRA And daily, as the sun ascends to noon,
The vot'ries still their pious visits pay.
But though no more the guilty court esteems
The God or worship, here Egysthus's spies,
Keep constant watch, and list with greedy ear,

E'en to the tenour of the pilgrim's prayer.
Retire my brother; shun their deadly sight;
Come when 'tis dark, and I will meet you then.

ORESTES I know the danger, but I trust the Gods
And my own destiny. Full well I know,
That the usurper, conscious of his crimes,
And dreading retribution, has contrived
A subtile and infernal enginry,
To crush the fruit of justice in the germ.

ELECTRA There's not a place it does not penetrate.
The sacred temples hold the tyrant's echoes.—
Know you, Egysthus has already heard
The number and equipment of your men?

ORESTES But of our enterprize he cannot know.

PYLADES Rumour is taught, that we advance ourselves
In quest of labours and romantic feats.

ORESTES Has not Egysthus heard of this?

ELECTRA He has.

ORESTES And laughs at us?

PYLADES Is it not so, Electra?

ELECTRA I never enter in the Tyrant's circle.
My feminine and simple pray'r is still,
That all your purposes may be for good,
And for their aim, be prosper'd by the Gods.

ORESTES What! though they mock at us, my dear Pylades,
They know us not, nor can their downward thoughts
Conceive the scope and motives of our daring.

Let them laugh on, while we pass to the goal
Of our magnificent and awful purpose.

ELECTRA But here, Orestes, do not linger now.
The very air is here a whisperer;
And as the viewless arrows of the pest,
The unknown ministers of vengeance speed,
And give the death before the victims feel,
Or fear themselves infected.—Stay not here.

ORESTES You must, Electra, then be spy for us.
The troops are waiting in the mountain pass,
With all prepared, the signals and the signs.
Pylades, safe in his disguise, will here
Attend your intimations. In the temple,
I will the anxious interval employ.

ACT I, Scene IV

ELECTRA *and* PYLADES.

ELECTRA Come, gentle cousin, let me lean on thee.
My heart shrinks in me. All the glowing joy
With which I heard Orestes was arrived,
Is changed into a chilling apprehension.

PYLADES Be more of heart; take courage from the hope
That leads our bold adventure. Rouse yourself
With the remembrance of your injuries.

ELECTRA I have so long on bitter sorrow fared,
That hope which should with chearfulness inspire,
Like heighten'd my disease. If ye should fail,
What may the fell usurper not attempt?
Already, from my lost unhappy mother,
His eye regardless roves; and I have felt
With sad abhorrence, his impassioned glance,
Flame on my conscious cheek.

PYLADES This day, Electra,
Will end your suffering and rebuild your fortune.

ELECTRA Yes; or forever desolate my hopes.
I was the worshipp'd daughter of a king,
But now I am below all slavery!

PYLADES Why yield you, gentle, to this sickly thought;
The cloud that has so long obscur'd your lustre,
Is swiftly passing, and the world again
Will own your regal brightness.

ELECTRA Ah Pylades;
Fortune may change the hues of outward show,
But cannot 'raze the truths engraven here.

PYLADES Ha! Who is this?

ELECTRA Egysthus! save yourself!

ACT I, Scene V

EGYSTHUS *and* ELECTRA.

EGYSTHUS Why turn you from me, and deny my sight,
The Heav'nly radiance of your gentle eyes?
What, though Orestes be no more?—

ELECTRA What he?

EGYSTHUS So says the rumour. Flesh is frail and mortal.
Nor tears, nor love itself that conquers all,
Can bribe the stern and greedy miser,
Death, E'er to unlock the coffer of the grave,
And give one jewel from his hoarded treasures.

ELECTRA When did he die? How came the tidings here?

EGYSTHUS 'Tis said, that he, gone errant with Pylades,
Fell in some battle near the spartan border.

ELECTRA If he fell nobly, he fell not too soon.
What is there here, in this rude world of time,
But shocks, and turbulence, and pain, and sorrow.

EGYSTHUS You seem content, nor look as one that hears
Such tidings of a brother. How is this?

ELECTRA He had but tasted bitterness and grief;
What joy had he to lose? What cause have I
To mourn for one that has escaped from woe?

EGYSTHUS Ah, pensive fair; could I but minister
To thy solace, and from this chance of fate,
Draw hope or comfort to a lover's heart!

ELECTRA What would you, sir? I pray you, let me pass.

EGYSTHUS Console you; and in symphony unite,
My kindest soothing to allay your sorrow.

ELECTRA My mother, sir, needs more your consolation.—
I pray unhand me, that I may retire?

EGYSTHUS Sweetest Electra, why so shy and perverse?
Why would'st thou tear from me, thy gentle hand?
Why, with thy scorn, so harshly wring my heart;
My wounded heart, that but thy smiles can cure!

ELECTRA Abhorr'd Incestuous! Heav'n! give me strength
To shake the monster from his loathsome hold.

EGYSTHUS This maiden artifice improves thy beauties.
Me-thinks the virgin glow upon thy cheek,
Deepens to ripeness, tempting to be gathered.—

O sure, these nimble sparklings of thine eyes,
Glance more of love than scorn.

ELECTRA Hence! dreadful man.
O Gods! by what unnat'ral transmutation
Of nature and of reason, does this wretch,
Foul with my father's blood, and from the couch
Of my ill-fated mother, newly risen,
Breathe this pollution in my tingling ears.

EGYSTHUS Less indignation, fair, disdainful maid.
Orestes' death leaves me free king of Argos,
And what I will, I may.—

ELECTRA Orestes' death!
Think'st thou, the righteous and tremendous Gods,
Had only him to be thy punisher?
Tyrant! beware and tremble; on thee fast
Rolls the inevitable vengeance down,
Like burning lava, dark, with clouds o'erspread.

ACT I, Scene VI

CLYTEMNESTRA *and* EGYSTHUS.

CLYTEMNESTRA Dearest Egysthus! now art thou all king.
The rabble vulgar, who refused the name,
Will, at the tidings of Orestes' death, Confer it freely.

EGYSTHUS Thou hast a stout heart,
To wear such blithesome ruddy on thy cheeks,
When tears should bleach them for a gallant son.

CLYTEMNESTRA Alas! you ill requite me. Oh! Egysthus,
The masterful and cherish'd love for thee,
Has drained the mother's nature from my breast.
Have I not doted so intensely on thee,

That all regard of duty, vows, and fame,
Have been as vile impediments push'd by,
That I might take thee with a larger grasp?

EGYSTHUS Come, come, dear wife; take not my words so sadly,
I meant no taunt.

CLYTEMNESTRA But I, with anxious pain, See oft thy eyes to other women stray.

EGYSTHUS No chidings, dame.—If this day's news prove true,
I'll make our Argos blaze, as bright again
As on your wedding-day with Agamemnon.

CLYTEMNESTRA Why name him to me? Oh! let him, Egysthus,
Lie quiet in that bloody sepulchre,
Where we, untimely laid him. His grim shade
That nightly visits my perturbed sleep,
Needs not the aid of your remorseless slight,
To barb its dread reproach.

EGYSTHUS What, penitent!
Now, this is but a woman's shallow trick,
To hide your jealousy. Dear Clytemnestra,
Love, once departed, will not come again,
By showing him the chaff of former fare.
Cupid has wings, the poets say, to fly:
Though, like the bee, he roves from flower to flower,
He will not always feed on cloying sweet.
Knowest thou, fair, that fondness may grow flat,
And smack of staleness too, yea turn to sour.
Come! learn philosophy; 'tis time you should.

CLYTEMNESTRA 'Tis time, indeed, when I am taught by you!

ACT II, Scene I

ORESTES

I am as one that swims a river's tide—
Swept by the stream, my efforts all in vain.
O that I never had been born! or that
The fate-controuling Deities had held
My mother from her crimes. Had she but shed
One glimpse of kindness on my helpless childhood;
One smile, such as the nursing menial smiles,
In simple-hearted fondness on the babe;
I might have felt some soft-restraining tie.
But Fate, which has with dreadful parricide,
Incarnadin'd my destiny, appears[41]
By the great plea of her deficiencies,
To blanch the horror of it from my mind;—
So large and universal has the want
Of all maternal been in her to me.

ACT II, Scene II

ORESTES, ELECTRA *and* PYLADES.

ORESTES How now Pylades? And Electra here!
Is this a time for wooing blandishments?
I thought my friend had been of purer mould,
Than in the turn and crisis of my life,
To yield to such soft weakness.

ELECTRA—Oh Orestes!—

ORESTES And thou too damsel, dar'st thou entertain
The smiling flatt'ry of a lover's suit,
While Heav'ns great ministers are all astir,
And on their thrones, th' eternal Gods themselves
Stand up expectant of a dreadful scene,—

---

41 *incarnadin'd*: to colour something a bright crimson or pinkish-red.

Th' avenging of thy sire? His restless shade
Walks round us here, and frowns to see thee thus.

PYLADES Forbear Orestes; this unjust reproach—
Electra seeks but to escape the foul
And insolent Egysthus.

ORESTES Say'st thou so?

ELECTRA Oft has he glanc'd from his presumptuous eyes
A fervent, strange familiarity,
That thrill'd in horror through my trembling frame.

PYLADES To-day embolden'd by the rumout'd fiction
Of our defeat and fall in Lacedemon,
He dar'd to give his hideous passion words.

ORESTES Lie quiet yet awhile, impatient Sword!
Thou see'st, Pylades, 'tis as I have said;
My destiny is clear. What monstrous shames
Are rife among us: but, the end is come.
Behold in Heav'n th' appointed sign display'd.
The sun is smitten with the promis'd darkness;
And when the gloom is rounded and compleat,
Then shall be done that dread predestin'd deed,
Which, ever sounding to the utmost time,
Will wake the echoes of posterity!

ELECTRA O ye deep-working and mysterious Powers!
That 'tend on nature, in this great probation,
Sustain my weakness.

PYLADES By what prescience,
Hast thou, Orestes, known the coming on
Of this portentous sign; thus to unite
This issue of our purpose and the omen?
Though we have grown from boyhood up together,
Shar'd the same sports, the same instruction drawn,

Slept in one chamber, at one table far'd,
And been in all things free and confident,
As if one mind our sev'ral natures sway'd,
'Till the first scheme of this thy high intent;
Thou dost my thoughts with wonder so amaze,
That while I should thee better know then others,
There is no other still so strange to me.

ORESTES Do you remember ought that chanc'd to us
Upon the day of that recorded night,
On which you swore to link your fate to mine,
In the great enterprize that brings us here?

PYLADES Were we not hunting the nemean boar,
With certain nobles of my father's court?

ORESTES Ay, and had pitch'd our tents upon the hill,
Fronting the sea-indented Salamis.

PYLADES I have the spot all painted in my mind.
'Twas scarce a bow-shot from the little temple,
Which an old mariner of Negara,
In gratitude for some escape at sea,
Had rais'd to Neptune and the God of day,
Serving their rites himself. And now I think,
You came not with us to the woods that day,
But went to see the hoary mariner.

ORESTES Him often since I have re-visited.

PYLADES When I return'd, I found you sad and moody,
And then it was you spoke of this design.

ORESTES That antient mariner had in his day,[42]
Seen many wonders of the sea and land,

---

42 Perhaps a reference to *The Rime of the Ancient Mariner* by Samuel Talyor Colleridge, published in 1798, a mere fourteen years before Galt penned Tragedies.

And learnt mirac'lous science. He had pass'd
Beyond th' Aurora of our western world,
To where the orient kings on opal walk:
And with the bold Phoenecians he had sail'd,
To where the long-foreseeing Druids teach
The untamed Britons, that within the oak,
The guardian spirit of their isle resides.
Deep was he vers'd in starry processes,
And could predict by hieroglyphic skill,
The fortunes and the accidents of men.
Seeing me thoughtful and diseased at heart
To be this offcast from the ties of nature,
He ey'd me kindly, often question'd me
With curious inquisition, and essay'd
To find if ever in my youthful breast,
Insidious Love had its sedition sown.
When he had found me honest, free and chaste,
He took his tablets, and by mystic signs,
And antique emblems keenly scrutinized,
Told me that fate had form'd me to avenge
My father's death, and Heav'ns justice deal
Against my guilty mother:—bidding me,
Momentous aspects of the air and sky,
Nightly to note; nor to advance myself,
Till thrice three hundred days were past and gone.
Then if my resolution lasted firm,
To be at Argos on this day prepar'd;
When glorious Phoebus in the bright of noon,
Would veil his light, in signal of approval.
And lo! the God assumes the gloom predicted!

PYLADES How was't you told me not of this before?
ORESTES My heart long doubtful, scarcely to this hour
Was nerv'd for the dread feat. But yon eclipse
Has all the wav'ring hues of hesitation,
By its deep influence fix'd in one black.

ELECTRA Ha! fly Orestes—hasten from this spot.
It is the queen that comes.

ORESTES—Oh! Gods! my mother!
Retire Pylades; let me look at her.

ACT II, Scene III

ORESTES *and* ELECTRA.

ORESTES Oh! that the Heav'ns should in a form so noble,
Have lodg'd a heart so foul. Majestic ruin!
Fain would I bend the filial knee before thee,
But the stern purpose that I come upon
Stifles the new-felt rev'rence as it stirs.
O mother, mother, did my melting soul
Retain one trace, but one of kindness from thee,
I would my terrible intent forego,
And at thy feet contend with destiny.

ACT II, Scene IV

CLYTEMNESTRA *and* ELECTRA. (ORESTES *apart.*)

CLYTEMNESTRA Canst thou unmov'd behold the God of day,
Shorn of his glory in the bright of noon?
The dark'ning prodigy still spreads apace.
The town is forth; and from the palace tower
The streets with wan and wond'ring faces seem
As thickly pav'd as with the wonted stones;
The cheek of life resigns the beauteous bloom,
And takes the ghastly ashy of the dead;
The hills frown black; the distant sea foregoes I
ts heav'nly azure for a dismal red;
The fields are chang'd, and for their cheerful green
Assume a sullen supernat'ral hue;
And solitary pasturing herds, in bands,
Come to the gates, and seek protecting man.

ELECTRA Portents and omens ever have been held
The harbingers of change. Yon black eclipse
Is but the forecast frown of some stern God,
In wrath descending for his rites profaned.
Now may the guilty quake.

CLYTEMNESTRA Whom dost thou mean? What guilty? Whom?
Dost thou mean me, Electra?

ELECTRA The conscious heart beneath such augury
Confesses to itself. You are the queen,
And ought to know; or knowing not should learn,
Why this portentous gloom appalling falls.[43]
The solemn Gods deal in no idle pageants.

CLYTEMNESTRA 'Twas but the chance of birth that made me queen.
I hold from nature no inheritance,
Above the frailties of the common race;
Food, sleep and pastime are as sweet to me,
As to the meanest slave that fears my frown.
Then why should I, so palpable to all
The ails and accidents of vulgar clay,
Believe that Heav'n takes stricter note of me,
Because my head sustains a glitt'ring toy,
And from my shoulders somewhat fuller hang
These two three spans of madder-tinctured robe,
Made from the cast-off mantle of a ewe!
I am a woman, made with woman's weakness.

ELECTRA My father, Agamemnon, wise men say,
Did, by the virtue of his great atchievements,
Exalt the aims and motives of mankind:
You! O my mother! were his honour'd wife.

CLYTEMNESTRA But he is dead; what is th' eclipse to him?

---

[43] The 1812 text has "appaling".

ELECTRA To him, 'tis true, all changes are alike;
The fears that shake us, and the ills that harm,
Effectless pass o'er his oblivious dust.

CLYTEMNESTRA Electra! wherefore do you taunt me so?

ELECTRA Alas! I only mourn my father dead.

CLYTEMNESTRA Maiden! how now? Dost thou forget thy mother?

ELECTRA Were you not too the mother of Orestes?

CLYTEMNESTRA Art thou my child, and dar'st upbraid me so?

ELECTRA The rude accuser wakes within yourself!
My heart weeps blood; and when I turn my eyes
To yon portentous blotting of the noon,
And think what dire reverse of moral nature
Reigns in our Argos, terror fills my breast.

CLYTEMNESTRA My child, my child, you sorely probe my heart;
Nor longer can I, to myself, appease
The terrible conviction of my guilt.
It flames before me, fierce as Phlegethon;
And now me-thinks I see, rising around,
The hideous brood of Acheron and Chaos,
Rearing their fiery snakes to drive me hence.—
Oh! my Electra, fain my blushing soul
Would make confession of its shame to thee;
But never can thy gentle spirit know,
The dreadful contest that is rending mine.
To-day, Egysthus, whose departed love
I long have miss'd, in many cold neglects,
Has scorn'd me openly, e'en while I felt
Unnat'ral joy, that, by Orestes's death,
He might possess an unmolested throne.

ELECTRA And he, to-day, made horrible my hearing,
With hideous proffer of detested love.

CLYTEMNESTRA Egysthus! love! did'st thou say, love to thee?
Art thou Electra, not the child I bore?—
O monster! monster! But all falls astray,
And noon turn'd night, is the least fearful change.
Strike! Heav'n, strike! and let me know no more.
Wilt thou submit thee to his curs'd embrace?
I'll tear thee from him like a hungry tyger;
Rive thee to joints; and on thy father's tomb,
Burn thy unhallow'd and incestuous bones,
To pacify the pale repining shade.
Oh! Agamemnon, thou art well reveng'd.

ELECTRA Orestes nears and waves me to retire.

ORESTES Hail Clytemnestra! royal murd'ress hail!

CLYTEMNESTRA Do I not dream; or what dread sounds are these?
Comes Agamemnon from the tomb to chide?

ORESTES Orestes' mother, hail! or by thy honour'd title,
Egysthus' dame! must I entice thy ear?

CLYTEMNESTRA Again, O Gods! he comes.

ORESTES Wilt thou not speak?

CLYTEMNESTRA What would's thou, restless and reproachful ghost?
I am prepar'd.—The spell of sin is o'er,
And Conscience wak'ning, wildly rings my doom.

ORESTES Where is thy son?

CLYTEMNESTRA Has he not joined thee yet?

ORESTES He comes! The mighty Gods themselves have plac'd
Their gleaming vengeance in his fated grasp.

CLYTEMNESTRA Oh! can my mis'ry yet such bitter want,
That I must fall by his unfilial arm?

ORESTES Did'st thou not first, these dire inversions prove?
Thou did'st, Unnatural! to-day, rejoice
In the reported death of this same son,
From whom thou dar'st to claim a mother's rights.
Behold how wide the reprobation works!
The glorious sun is fading to a blot
In the mid Heav'n of noon, as if he shunn'd
The pestilence which thy example lewd,
Has rais'd in Argos. Know'st thou not, to-day,
That thy Egysthus; thy fam'd spouse! Egysthus,
Has breath'd the loathsome fervor of his love
To thy own daughter? Yet thy doting eyes
Look on him fondly.

CLYTEMNESTRA Cease, perturbed shade.
To-day, forever from my tortur'd bosom,
I cast him forth; and penitence and woe,
For all the wretched remnant of my life,
Shall feed upon me, till my wasted frame
Has done atonement for its guilty passion.

ORESTES Infirm and fleeting that contrition is,
Which shame of mortified denial breeds.
Springs thine from hatred of thy own desires?

CLYTEMNESTRA Thy scrutinizing inquisition, shows
A fearful glass to my convicted soul.—
I dare not look on my deformity.
Upbraid no more, but with thy deadly hand,
Seize and convey me to thy shadowy home.

ORESTES Then yield thyself.

CLYTEMNESTRA O Gods!

ELECTRA She faints; help! help!

ACT II, Scene V

CLYTEMNESTRA, ELECTRA, *and* EGYSTHUS.

CLYTEMNESTRA Oh! my Electra; and is it away?

EGYSTHUS What Clytemnestra?

CLYTEMNESTRA Ha! com'st thou here too?
Avaunt! abhorr'd: there's torment in thy touch.
Hence! lest the awful and vindictive ghost,
Transform itself into wide-wrapping flame,
And mix our ashes in one sudden doom.

EGYSTHUS What can she mean, Electra?

CLYTEMNESTRA Is it so?
And dar'st thou woo her in my very sight?
Blaze forth again to vision, dreadful child,
From the enchanting venom of his tongue.—
Deem not thy virtue firmer than thy mother's;
For I was bound by holy charm of vows,
To one whose name should have been charm enough,
Against the conjurations of the sense.
Sure, I was drawn, by worse than sorcery,
To plot my husband's death, and drench my sleeves
Deep in the flowing ruby of his blood.
E'en now thy father, all magnificent,
Before me stood, as when he sail'd for Troy:
His armour sounding as he mov'd along
Tow'ring refulgent. In his searching eyes,

Me-thought a sad and wat'ry pity hung,
That kindly mercified their angry fires.

EGYSTHUS 'Twas but a phantom of thy fever'd fancy:
The self same substance as the nightly dreams
That chace thy needful sleep.

CLYTEMNESTRA Beware, Egysthus; yet repress the smile
That grows to mock'ry on thy jutting lip.
Such visitations are not idly made;
And see the sun on his meridian throne,
Spreads a black signal to the world of men.

ACT III, Scene I

PYLADES *and* ORESTES.

PYLADES By the time it should be nigh the noon of day,
But night portentous has usurp'd the sky.
All birds are bower'd save witching Hecat's bird,[44]
 The bat that, in its murky flutter, shrieks
A shrill amen to the ill owlet's bode.
The sun has dwindled to an edge of light,
And seems the glitt'ring remnant of a ring.
Heav'n's lamps as in the midnight are lit up:
But in the preternatural reverse,
That seizes all; their constellated fires
Present the aspect of th' autumnal sky.

ORESTES How now, Pylades! art thou stricken too?

PYLADES In truth, Orestes something much like fear,
Chilly and pale upon my fancy creeping,
Daunts from my heart its wonted confidence.

---

44 Hekate / Hecate, the Greek goddess of magic, witchcraft, the night, moon, ghosts and necromancy.

ORESTES Bear up man, and take courage from the sign;
It suits our awful enterprize, and shows
The Gods auspicious. What we aim to do,
Is such a deed that, with less sanctioning,
We might have deem'd it of another stamp.
But all these pageants of the ominous sky,
Prove that the Heav'ns have interest in our purpose.

ACT III, Scene II

ORESTES, ELECTRA *and* PYLADES.

ORESTES My sister! how is this? What would'st thou here?
This is no place now for thee to abide.
The troops are posted.—To thy room again;—
Our business ill thy gentle nature suits.

ELECTRA O my Orestes! let me stay with thee.
Alone I dare not trust my busy thoughts.
Unutterable fears, suggestions dire,
And cogitations of unhallow'd scope,
In spite of reason glide into my mind.
All seems unnat'ral, e'en the Gods are serv'd
With rites and worship reprobate and grim.
The glorious Phoebus, like dark Hecaté,
Is hail'd in orgies ghastly and obscure:
The fearful crowds with torches glaring flame,
Rush to his temple; howling and sad cries
Are heard for tuneful hymns; and clotted gore
Of felon victims, manacled with iron,
Dragg'd from the dungeons and in fury torn,
Besmear the silver altars of the God.

PYLADES Gentle Electra droop not so dismay'd.

ORESTES You know not yet the soul-inspiring cheer
Of these celestial assurances.

By such dread prodigies in heav'n and earth
Mysterious providence controuls mankind.⁴⁵
Let no one say such things are negative.

ELECTRA Thy mind, dear brother, teems with dark conceits.
I understand thee not, or wish I may not.

ORESTES Go to thy chamber, and abide our call.
Pylades lead her.—I will to the men,
Lest they too catch the horror of the time.

ACT III, Scene III

ELECTRA *and* PYLADES.

ELECTRA I will not go, Pylades; rather here
Let me be witness to the worst I think,
Than haunted by the demon of my fears.
O that I could but freely speak to him!
But when I would he seems to look on me,
With such endurance as a mother views,
The aimless pastime of her ideot child.⁴⁶

PYLADES What would you say to him? would you restrain
The mighty justice that has brought him here?

ELECTRA I think Orestes has a mind most noble?—

PYLADES Truly so, and virtuous passing man.

ELECTRA 'Tis but the height of his stupendous worth,
That breeds in me this terrible alarm.

PYLADES He to the acts of his decided purpose,

---

45 The spelling of "controuls" is Galt's affectation of archaic language.
46 Again, the spelling of "ideot" appears to be Galt's affectation of archaic language.

Moves with the equanimity of Jove.
Sweet! what is this? Why spring these sudden tears?

ELECTRA When the heart's full the eyes will overflow.—
Alas! that I should yield to such conceits.
PYLADES To what, Electra?

ELECTRA Ever to suspect
The sanctity of his superior nature.
Why should his heav'nly magnanimity
Beget in me this fear.

PYLADES Fear! how? What fear?

ELECTRA O why, Pylades, does his moody thought
Seem less against the doom'd Egysthus bent,
Than on the guilt of his unhappy mother;
And this magnificence of sign and omen?

PYLADES He views Egysthus as the murd'rous knife:
But Clytemnestra was the urging hand.

ELECTRA O that he were not so juridical!—
You are his friend, his bosom friend, Pylades;
The full confided partner of his thoughts—

PYLADES Ha! wherefore trembling grasp you thus my arm.

ELECTRA Answer me truly.

PYLADES—What would you, Electra?

ELECTRA Oh sure, Oh sure, we have had crimes enough.

PYLADES Alas!—

ELECTRA Then it is so!—O gentle Death!
Shut up my sense from this catastrophe.

ACT III, Scene IV

ORESTES, PYLADES, *and* ELECTRA.

ORESTES Still here, Pylades! with Electra here!
How now Infirm! Is this thy vow to me?
And thou, pale girl, why would'st thou wond'ring stand
In the great thoroughfare of Fate and Death?
Hence to thy distaff or to pray'r. Pylades,
Look how the sun is to a twinkle shrunk.
When all is quench'd to our terrestrial vision,
I'll strike upon my shield. Be you prepar'd,
For at the signal's sound, the men, behind
The colonades, will to the storming rush.

ELECTRA Orestes, O my brother!—

ORESTES How! still here!
Into the temple, child, or to thy chamber.
Here is no place for thee, nor time for words—
Ha! who are these that from the palace come?—
Swift to thy post, Pylades—I to mine.

ACT III, Scene V

ELECTRA.

O ye dread deities, this work is yours!
It is my wretched mother, and Egysthus,
Sent helpless here for their own sacrifice;
With all the train of the pliant priests that gave
A guilty acquiescence to their sin.
Alas! alas! with what despairing looks,
She frequent turns, and eyes the blacken'd sun:
Herself too chang'd from all imperial show.

ACT III, Scene VI

CLYTEMNESTRA, EGYSTHUS, ELECTRA, *Priests and Torch-Bearers.*

CLYTEMNESTRA Electra, O Electra, stand'st thou here
With thy undaunted innocence to shame us!
Look on her now, and if thou can'st, Egysthus,
Beneath these dismal prodigies of Heaven,
Find courage still to love, now woo and win.

ACT III, Scene VII

CLYTEMNESTRA, EGYSTHUS, ELECTRA, ORESTES, *and* PYLADES.

CLYTEMNESTRA Ha! Agamemnon, come again to chide!—

EGYSTHUS Who? What art thou?

ELECTRA O mother, 'tis Orestes.

EGYSTHUS Orestes! and alive!

CLYTEMNESTRA 'Twas then no vision!

EGYSTHUS Guards! guards!

ELECTRA Fly, mother, fly.

CLYTEMNESTRA Am I awake!
What means this clang, like Jove's own thunder peal?

EGYSTHUS Has he sown here the Theban's dragon teeth,
That these grim soldiers in full panoply,
Start up around us like an apparition?

ORESTES Pylades seize him!

EGYSTHUS First secure thyself.—

ORESTES Audacious dog! and darest thou strike at me?

CLYTEMNESTRA Spare him, Orestes, O in mercy spare—

ORESTES Ill-fated sure art thou to use the word!
Mercy to him by whose accursed stroke,
My royal father in his glory fell!
Mercy to him by whose detested wiles,
My mother was unmother'd to myself!
Mercy to him who with incestuous pray'r,
Did the chaste hearing of thy child amaze!
No: cruelty by every fury mixt.—
Die monster, die!—Now murderess prepare—

ELECTRA Pylades! O Pylades! yet arrest—

CLYTEMNESTRA Orestes! son! what would'st thou do to me?—

PYLADES O stay, O stay, the parricidal blow.—
If the dread Gods for their offended justice
Demand atonement, they have power to take,
Without the horror of thy agency.
'Tis not for thee, so knit by the great ties
Of blood and nature, thus, for her offence,
To bear the warrant, or to strike the doom.

ORESTES Pylades! when I first proposed to thee,
This work of justice that we now perform,
Thou did'st, by all the deities of Light,
And each particular energy of Hell,
Nam'd one by one, swear to proceed with me,
To the extremest verge of my intent,
As willing, ready, and commandable
As this my own right hand. Such was thy oath.

PYLADES It was, Orestes; but my fancy never
Conceiv'd the aim of thy revenge was this.

ORESTES Does the right hand remonstrate with the will?
Does it make wherefores at its work?
Were I To bid thee, in this wretched woman's bosom,
Strike deep the irremediable dagger;
Art thou not bound to do't?

PYLADES Oh! my Orestes,
Put not upon me such a dreadful task.

ORESTES Thou wast too valiant in thy vow, Pylades!
Turn my Electra, turn thy head aside:
Thou hast not courage to behold the blow.

CLYTEMNESTRA Strike! strike, at one, nor torture with delay.[47]

ELECTRA O look, Orestes, where Egysthus lies,
Stiff'ning in death and clotted with his gore.
No more to him can our ill-fated mother
Relapse in fondness; spare her then to mourn
The woeful issue of her fatal passion;—
In piety for her contrition, spare.

ORESTES Thou hast assail'd me with a painful weapon.

PYLADES Yield! yield, Orestes, to this thaw of nature.

ORESTES Mother!

CLYTEMNESTRA O Gods!

ORESTES They wait the sacrifice.

---

47 A comma is placed at the end of this line in the 1812 text, I have replaced that with a full stop.

CLYTEMNESTRA Oh! fatal scion, of a fated stock,
Whose fruit has still been misery and crime;
Is't not enough that I am crimson deep,
With the brave blood of my heroic lord,
But that my own must curse my offspring too!
Hold! impious youth; in thy stern purpose, stay;
Think what a claim a parent may put in:
'Tis true that Agamemnon was thy sire;
But am not I thy mother, and may urge
As just a plea as the lamented dead.

ORESTES If thou hast on me that imperious claim,
Which tender mother's o'er their children hold,
Then set it forth as I recount to thee,
The duties that were thine. The bleating babe,
By mystic Nature, naked and defenceless,
Is to the mother's charities commended,
As much as by the conscious tie of birth.
What gentle office hast thou done for me?
Hast thou e'er follow'd, with thy hands outstretch'd,
In anxious joy upon my tott'ring childhood;
Watch'd the first glimpses of my opening mind;
And by a wide and all-surrounding love,
In soft refraction bent the rays on good?
Close as the general interposing air,
Is the true mother's anxious vigilance,
Around her child: but where was thine to me?
As to the bird the shell, thou wast my mother:
All cherish, watch, and gentle care were waiting;
And as vile excrescence well remov'd,
I was cut off, and destined to destruction.

CLYTEMNESTRA Thou speaking conscience, cease! upbraid no more.
If thou wilt spare me, Oh! in pity, cease.
Upon her knees, thy weeping mother see;
She craves for life, to spend that life in woe.

ORESTES Where was thy pity for my noble sire?
Where were thy tears when he before thee lay,
Slain victim to thy odious deity, The rank Tisiphoné?[48]

CLYTEMNESTRA Alas! Orestes.—
Yawn thou firm earth, and give me room to hide
From this tremendous and avenging fiend.

ELECTRA Oh! to the temple, to the temple fly.

PYLADES Orestes, stay; thy kindling rage restrain.

ORESTES Away! weak girl. Dar'st thou Pylades too?—
Th' eclipse is full!—Who follows me shall die.

ACT III, Scene VIII

ELECTRA *and* PYLADES.

ELECTRA Oh! coward priests, will you not after him,
Nor save e'en your own altars from the strain?
Pylades too! canst thou stand shiv'ring here?—
O Gods! O Gods! Orestes! Oh! my brother!
Rise! rise dread spirit of my father, rise!
And scare him from the crime. Egysthus! wake!
Hast thou no ghost to blaze upon his sight?
Oh! ye that rule the influential stars,
Strike down with palsy his uplifted arm! Pylades!
Oh Pylades!—Hark! hark! hark!

PYLADES 'Tis but the solemn sounding of his tread.

ELECTRA Comes he yet back?

PYLADES Not yet.

---

48 One of the ancient Greek Furies, she punished crimes of murder: parricide, fratricide, and homicide.

ELECTRA What sounds are these?

PYLADES A wail and general lamentation spreads
Through all the city.

ELECTRA List.—Did you hear that?

ORESTES *On to the altar; to the altar straight!*

CLYTEMNESTRA *Murderer! matricide, forbear! forbear!*

ORESTES *The priest of Justice for his victim waits.*

CLYTEMNESTRA *Ho! you without; will no one help? Help! help!*

ORESTES *All now were vain.*

PYLADES O Heav'ns! she falls, she dies.—
'Tis past, Electra; see th' avenger comes,
With ghastly horror, and all grim with gore.

ACT III, Scene IX

ORESTES, ELECTRA, PYLADES, &c.

ORESTES Now it is done: and lo, the sun again
Emerges from the gloom. Softly around
Breaks forth a joyous universal hail;
Why then, Electra and Pylades dear,
Stand ye so mute, and look on me so strange?
Come, my sweet sister, let me lead thee hence.
We are two orphans, and in all the world,
Were never woeful orphans more forlorn.

ELECTRA Horrible sight! thy breast is foul with blood;
Thy mother's blood!—Release me awful man.

ORESTES What, my Pylades! where's thy gratulation?
Give me thy hand.

PYLADES Oh! what is this?

ORESTES My dagger!
Hence! blushing weapon.—Oh! could but the sight,
So soon, a sworn and sacred friendship sever!
Take her, Pylades, she has clung to thee.
'Tis I, 'tis I alone, that am the orphan.
But fare ye well; me no fond link detains;
I have the world's spacious range before.
Cast out in childhood from my mother's breast,
Fate from the birth, has destin'd me to be
This general denizen; then why should I,
At your amaz'd and chilling looks repine.
Friends! why is this? They shake their heads and sigh;
And, to the temple, gaze, with sad enchantment.
What see they there?—Pylades, save me! save me!
See! see! where o'er my bleeding mother's corse,
The snake-hair'd furies of perdition stand.
They come, they come, in flaming rage upon me!
Ha! Here too! Others! Whither shall I fly?

END.

www.ingramcontent.com/pod-product-compliance
Lightning Source LLC
Chambersburg PA
CBHW031144160426
43193CB00008B/251